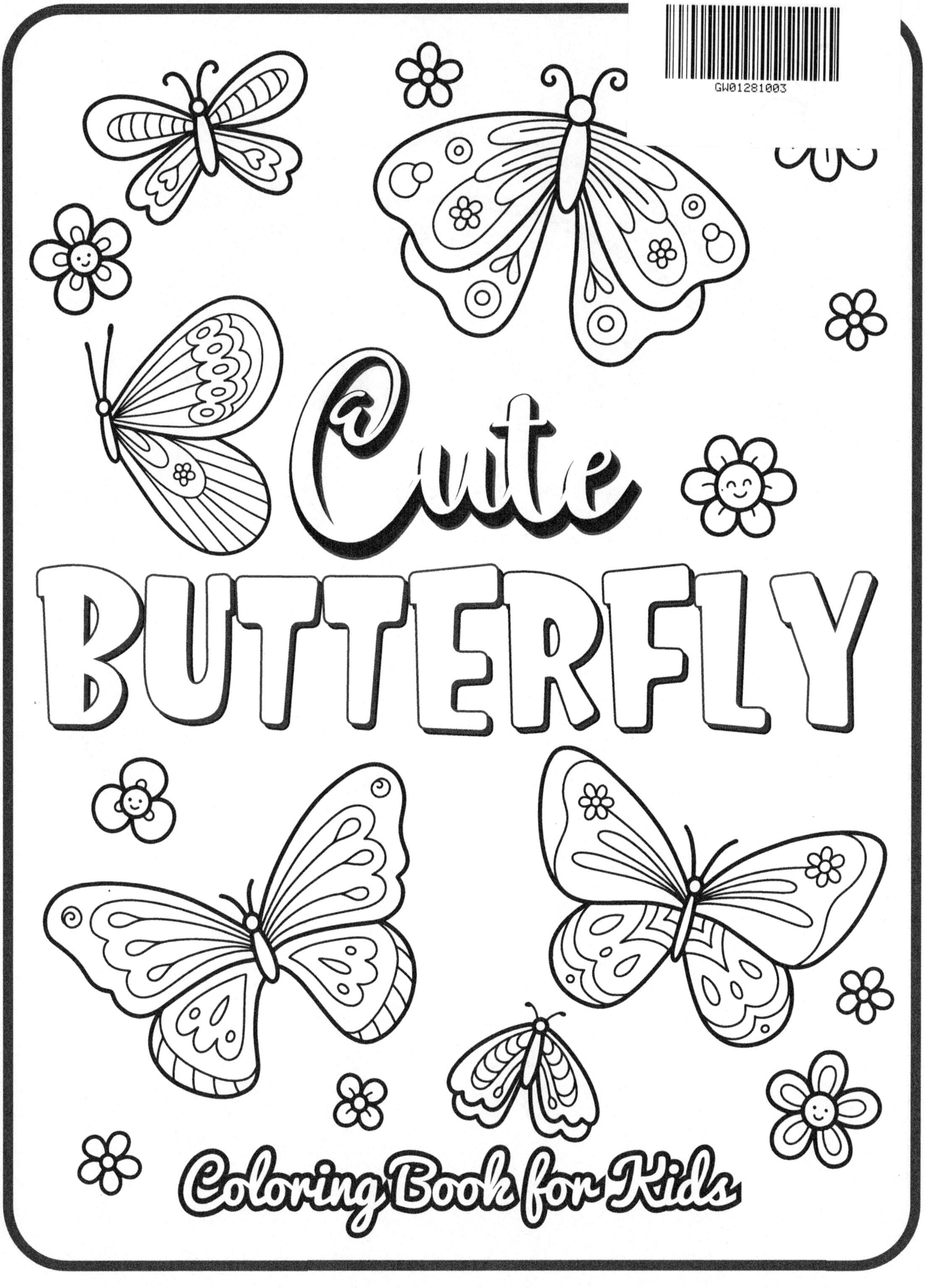
Cute
BUTTERFLY
Coloring Book for Kids

This Book Belongs To :

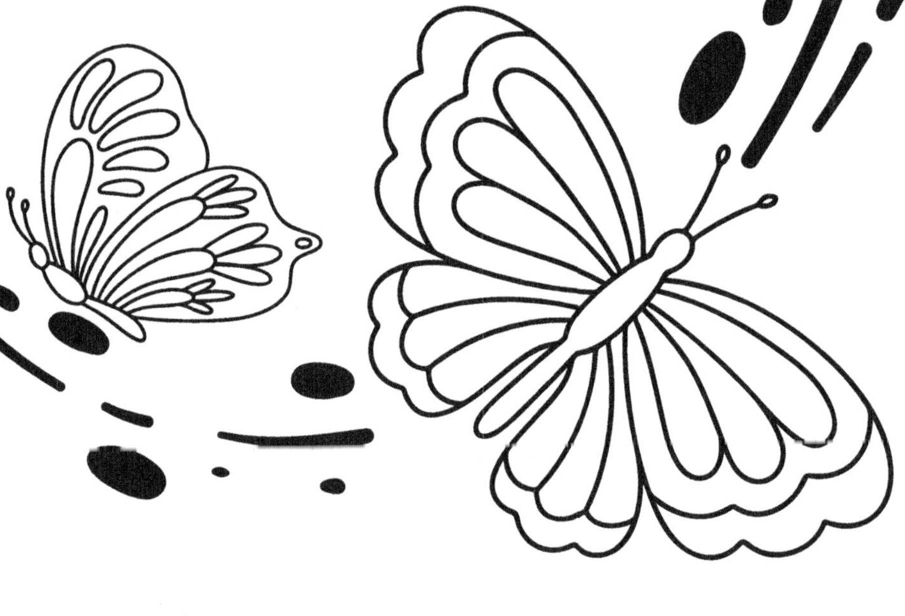

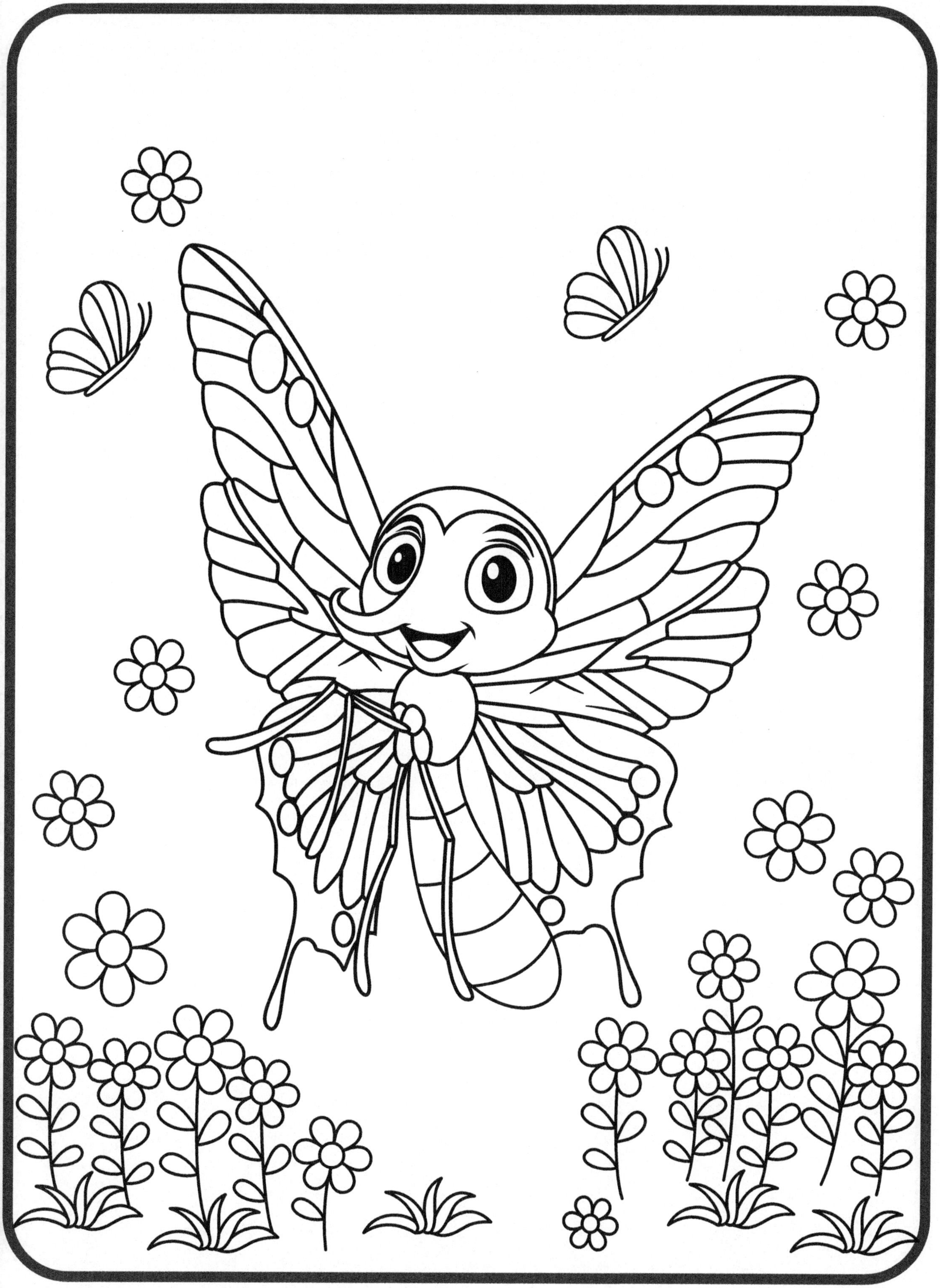

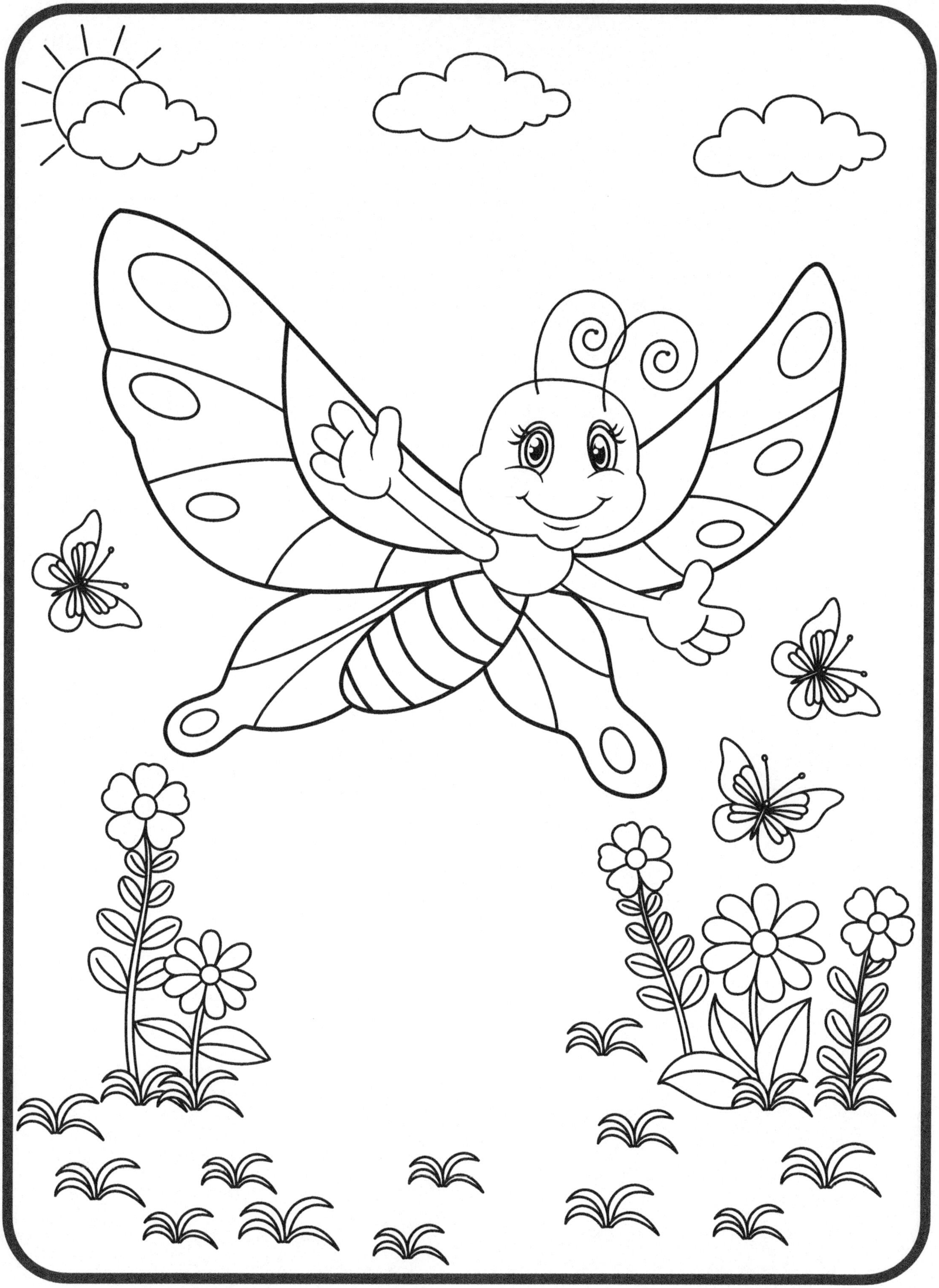

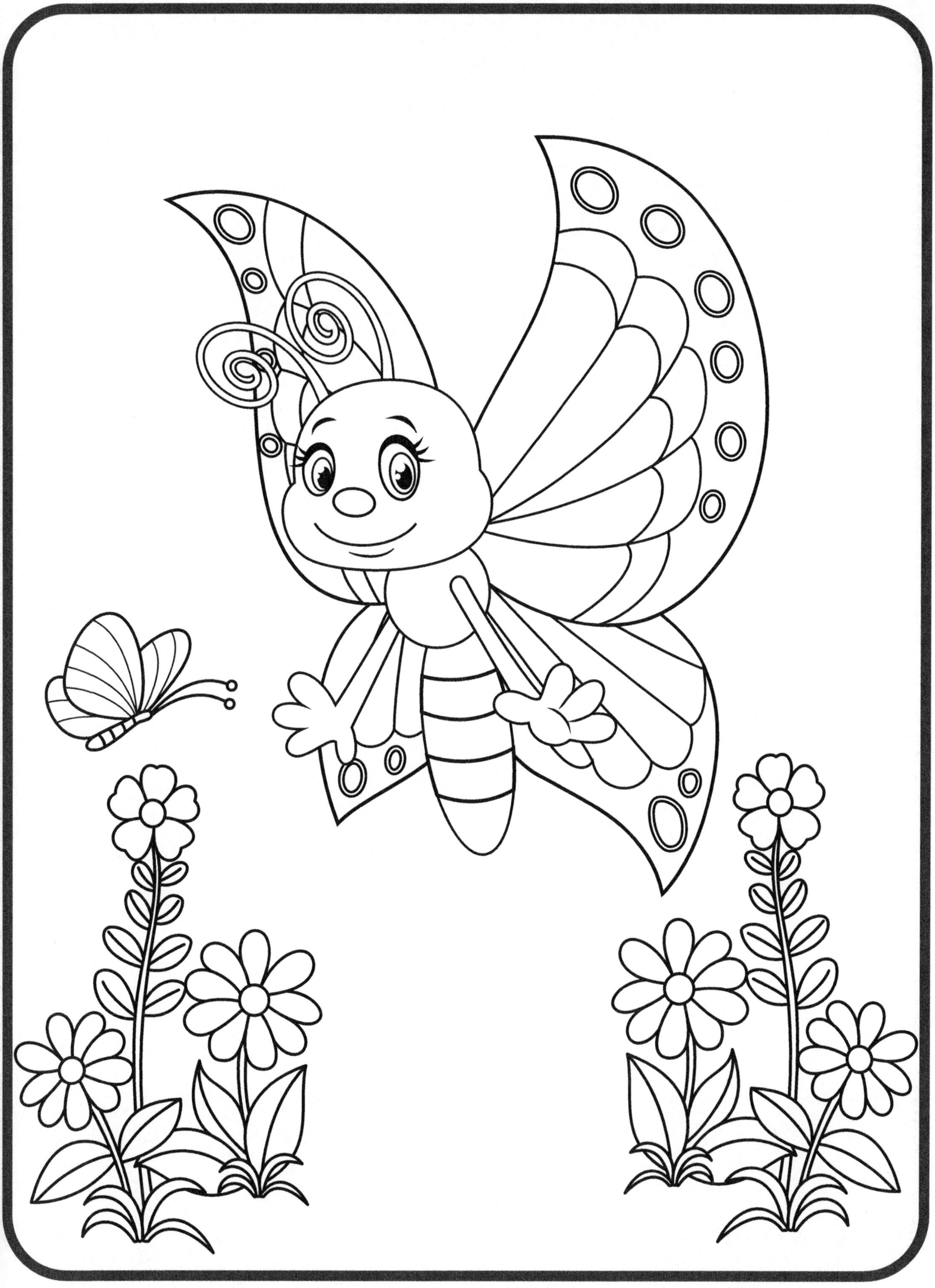

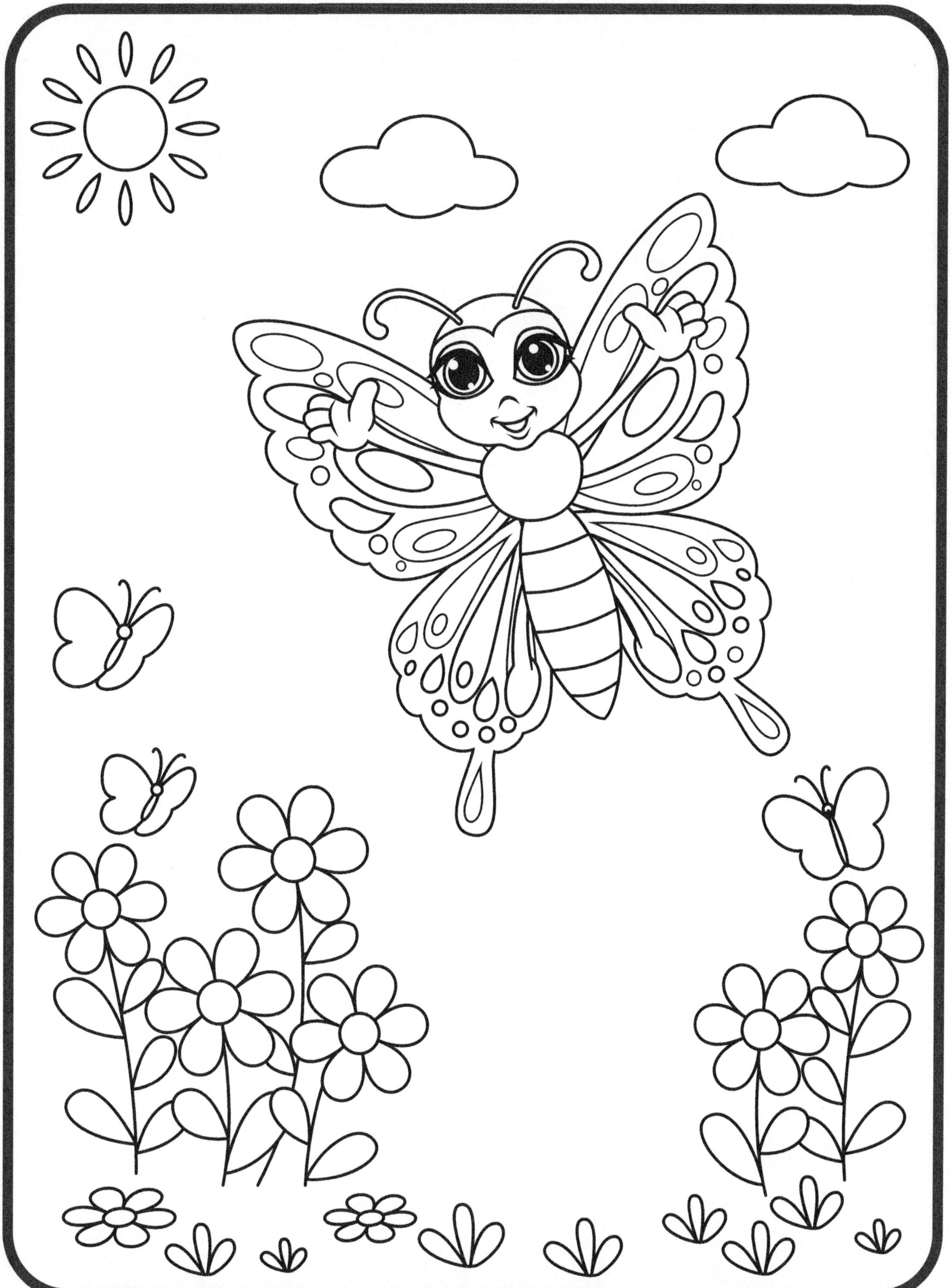

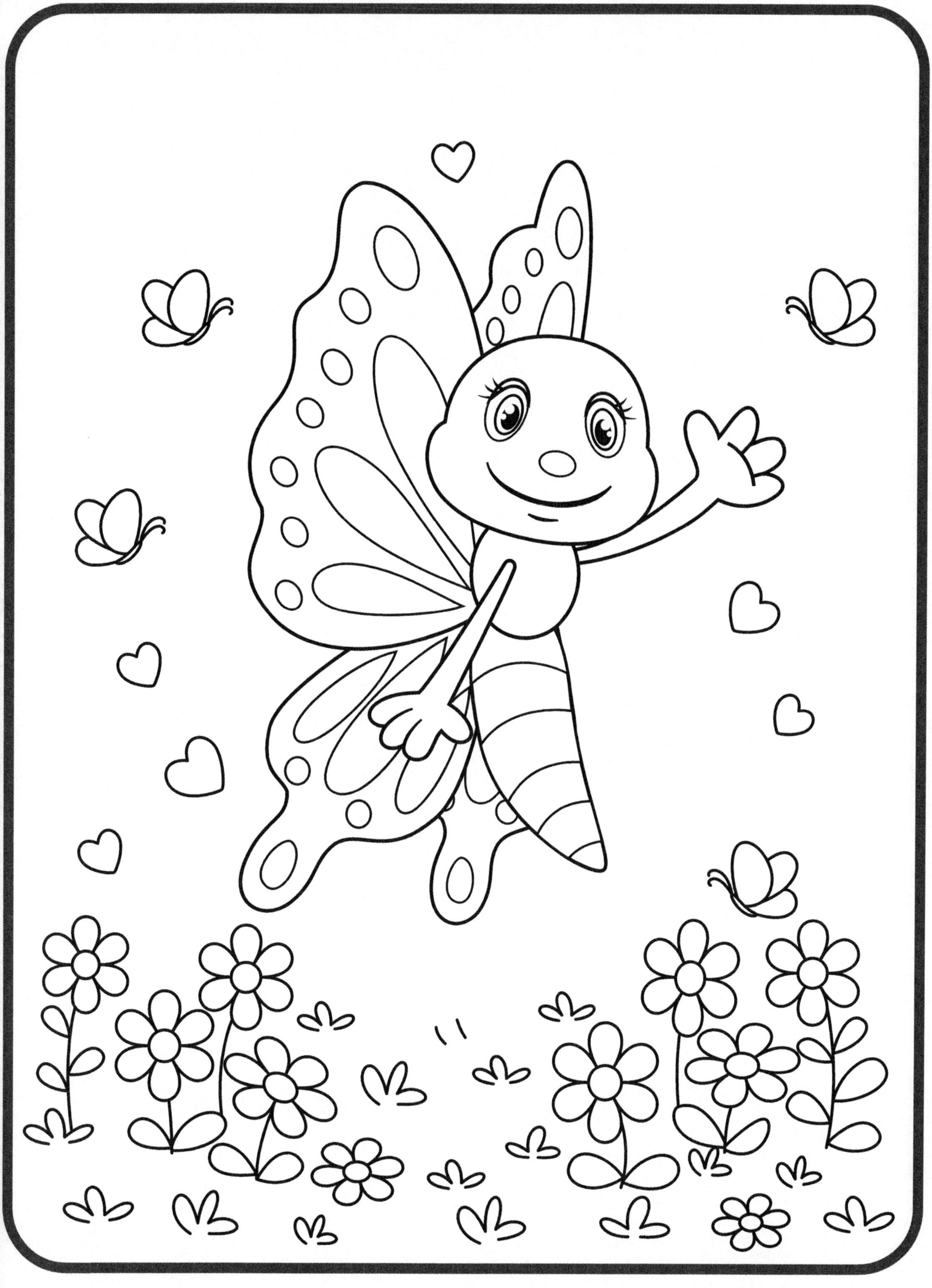

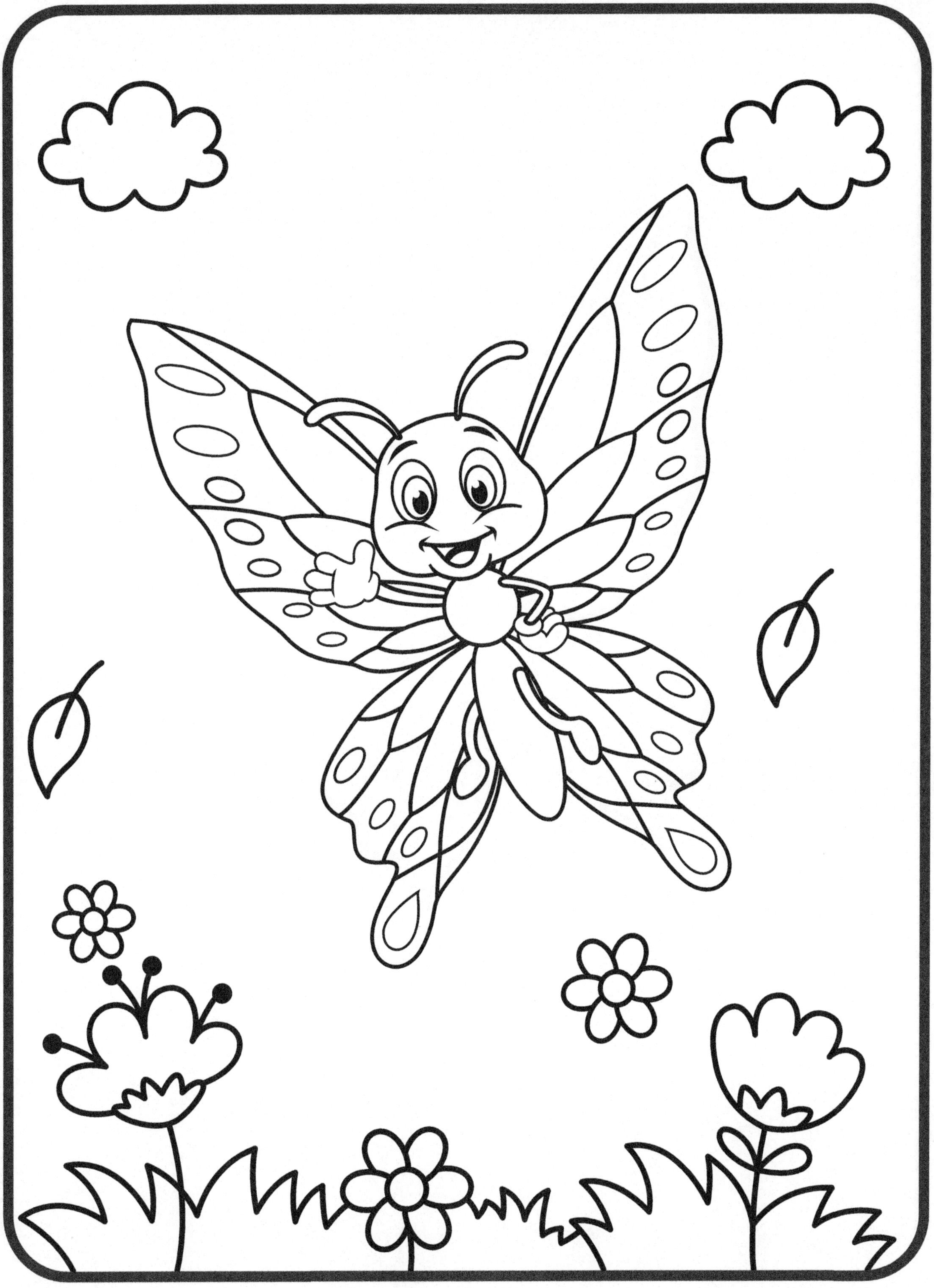

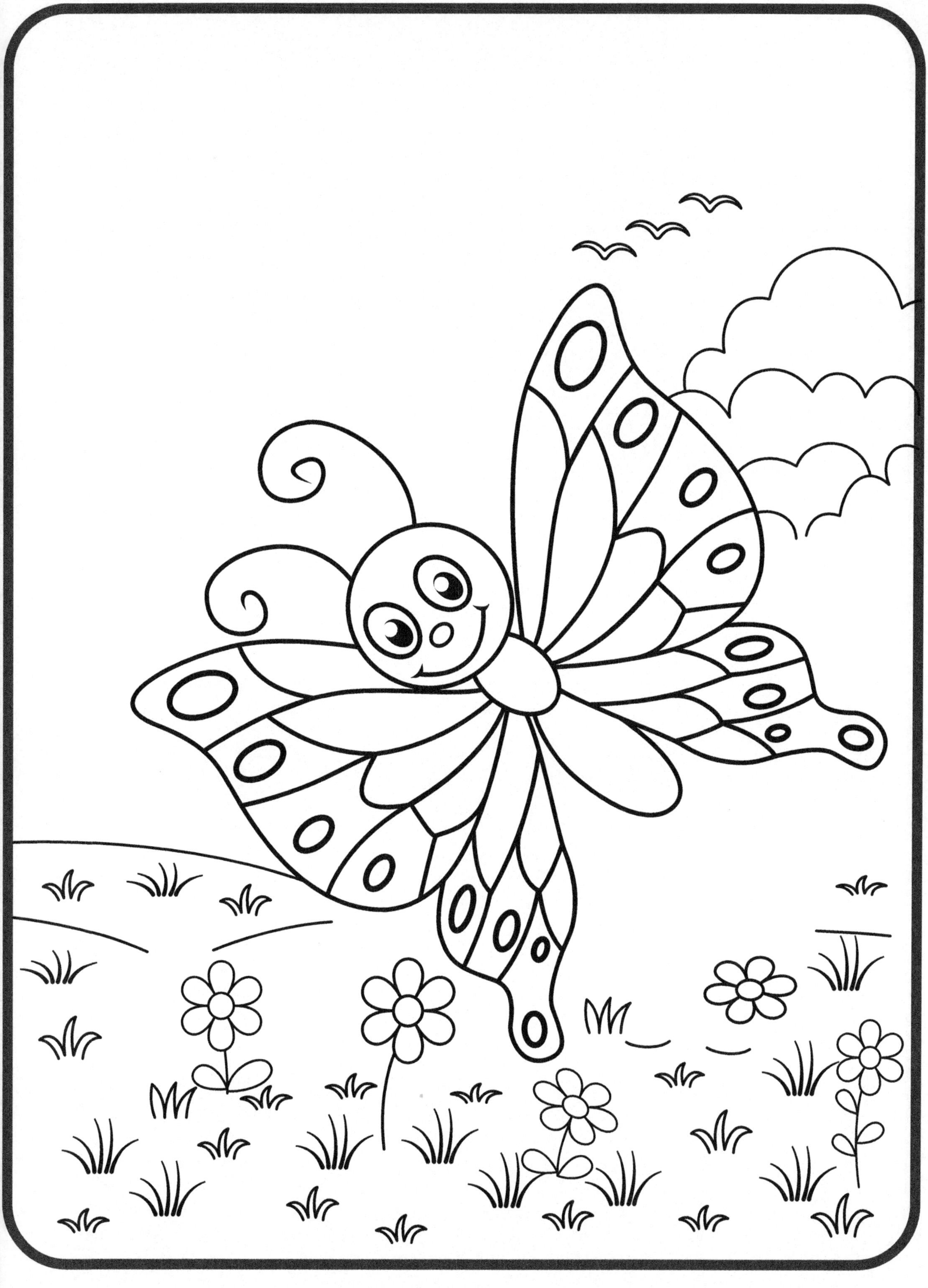

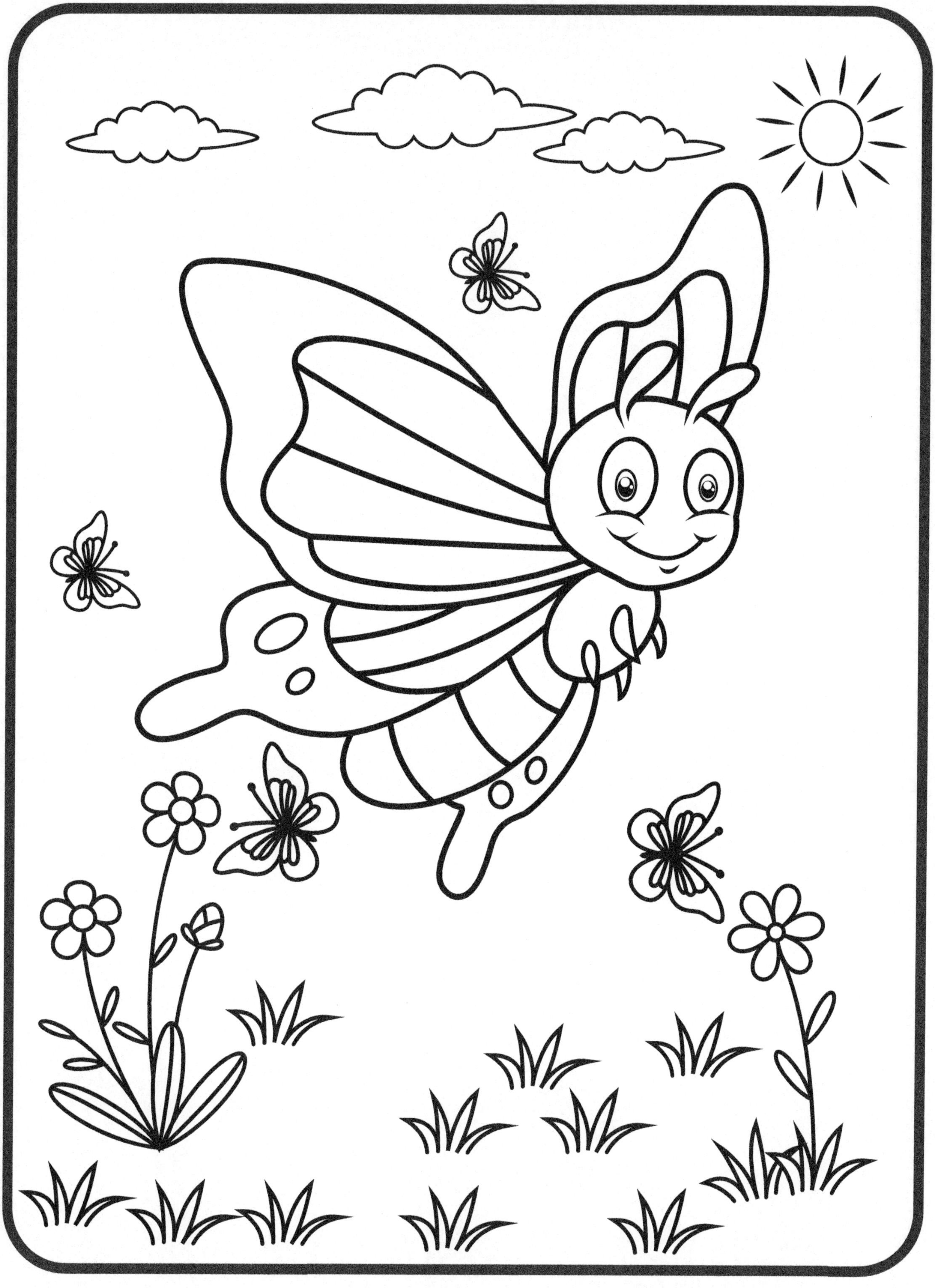

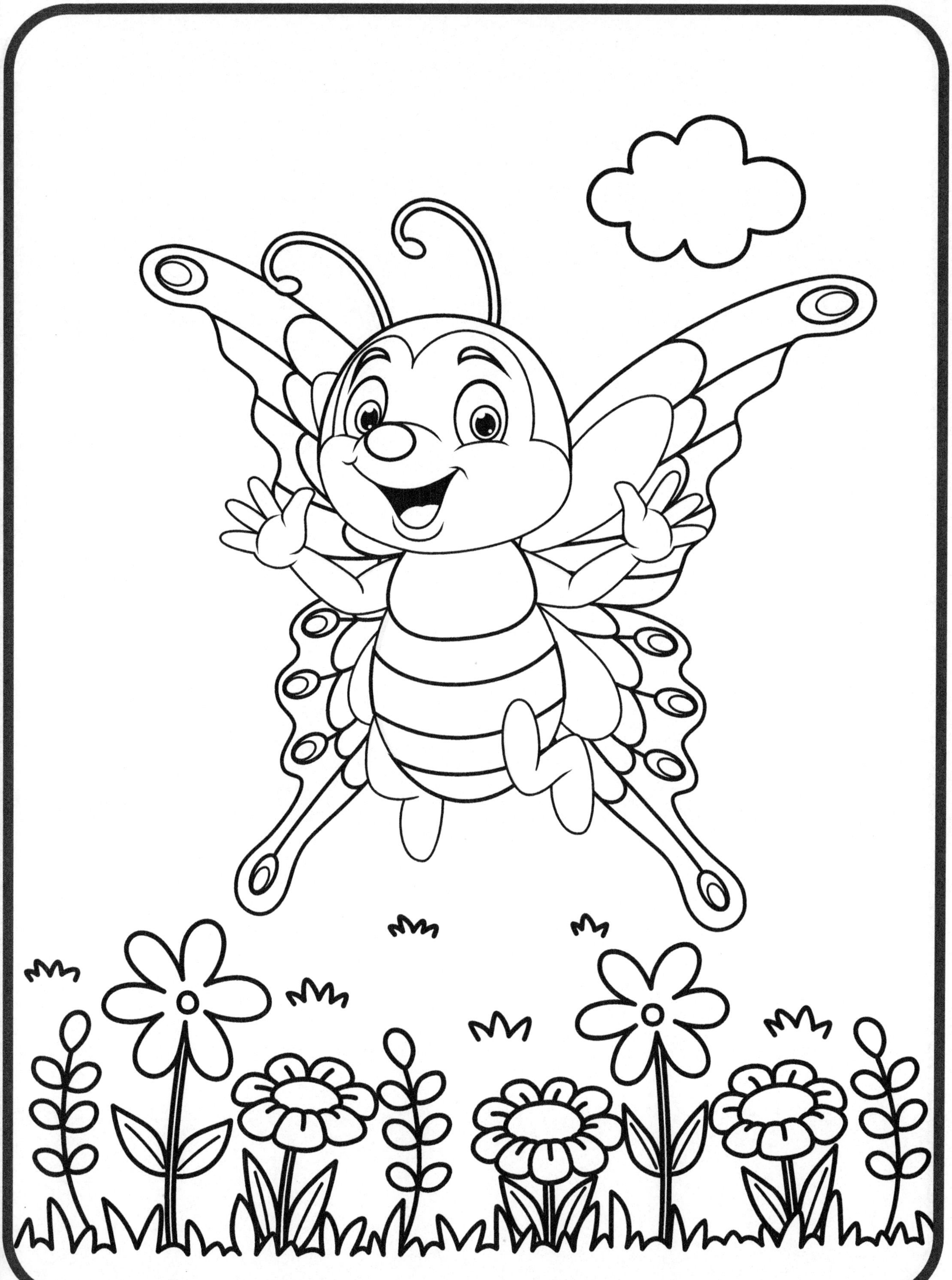

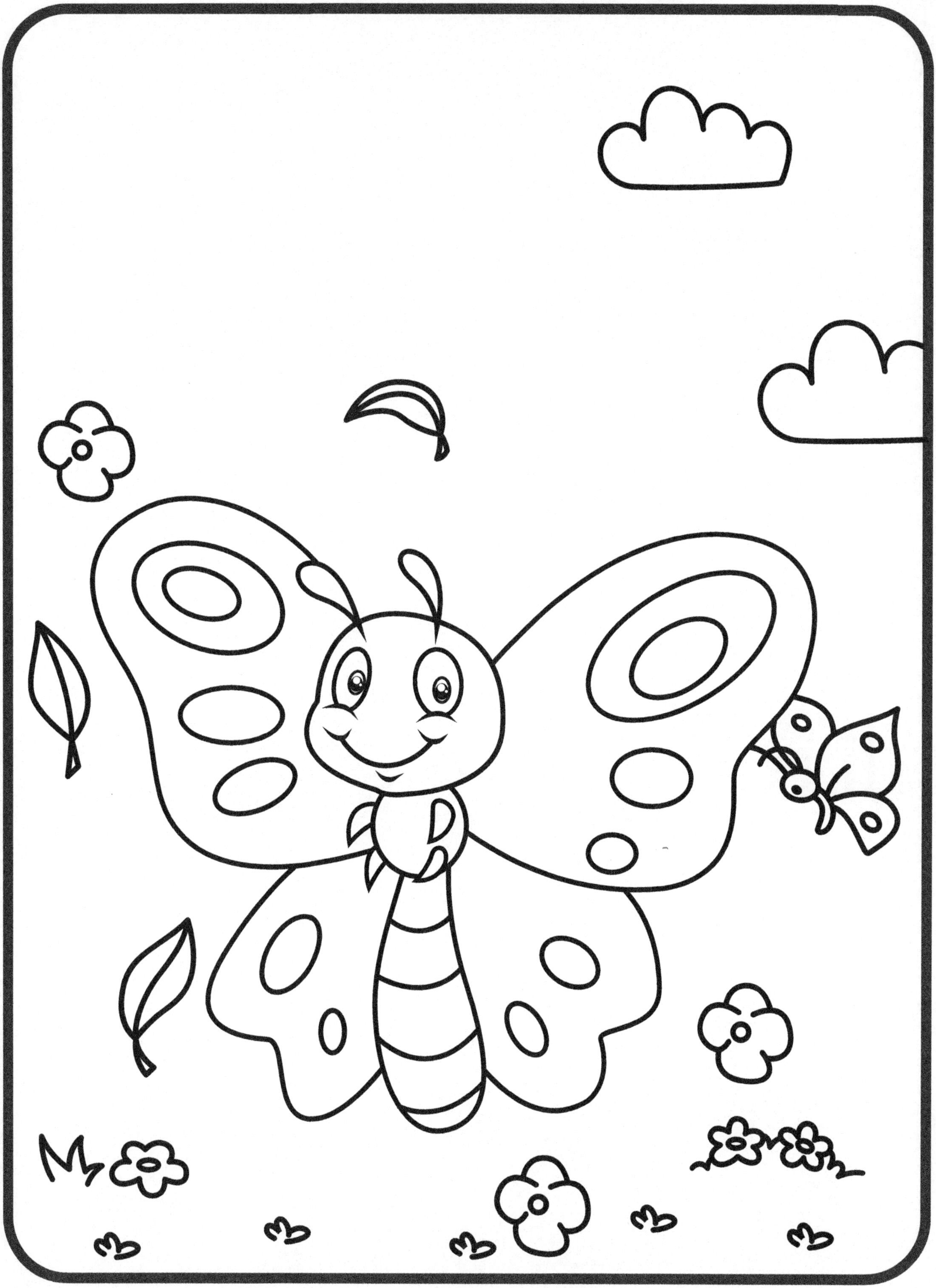

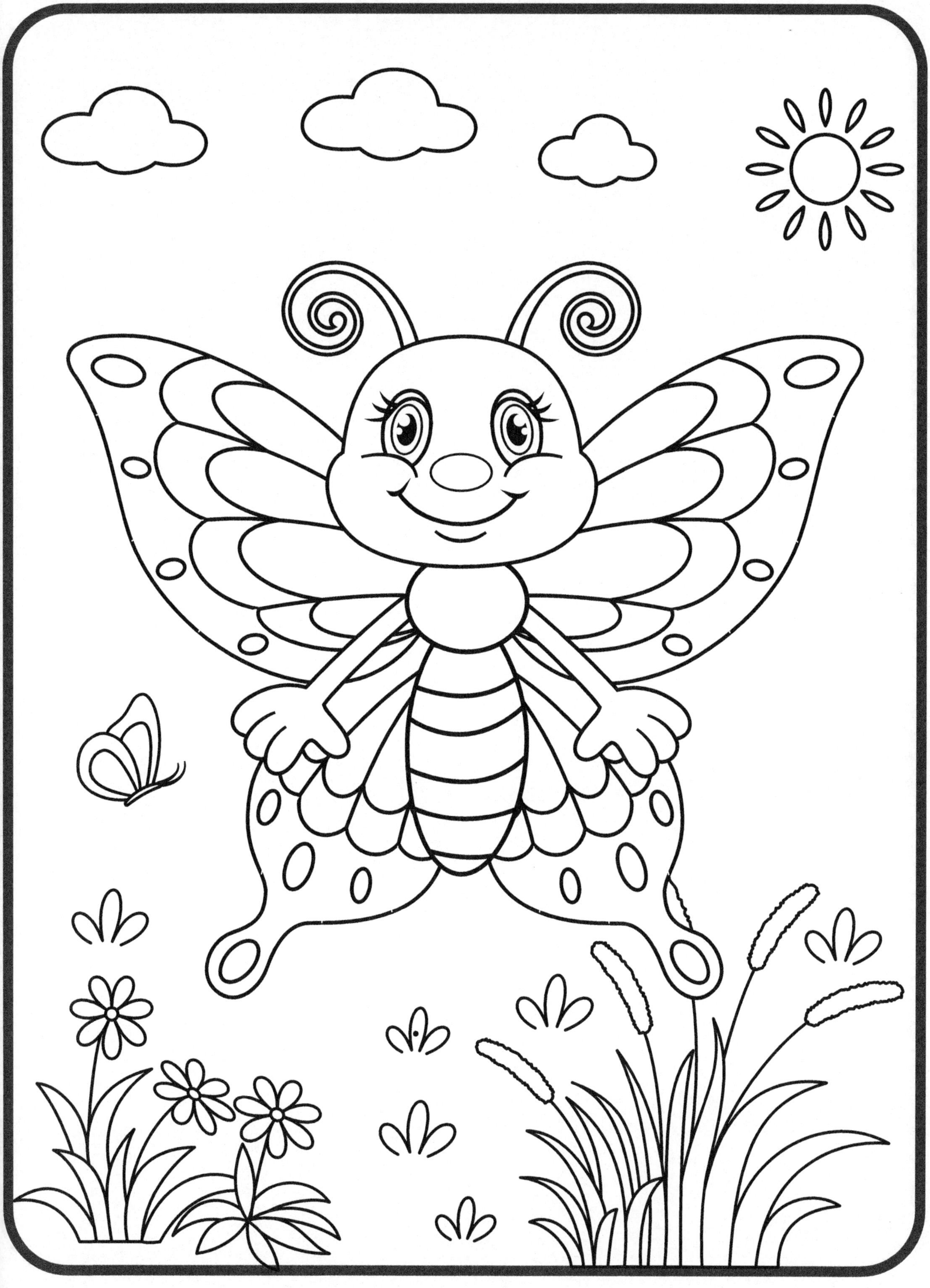

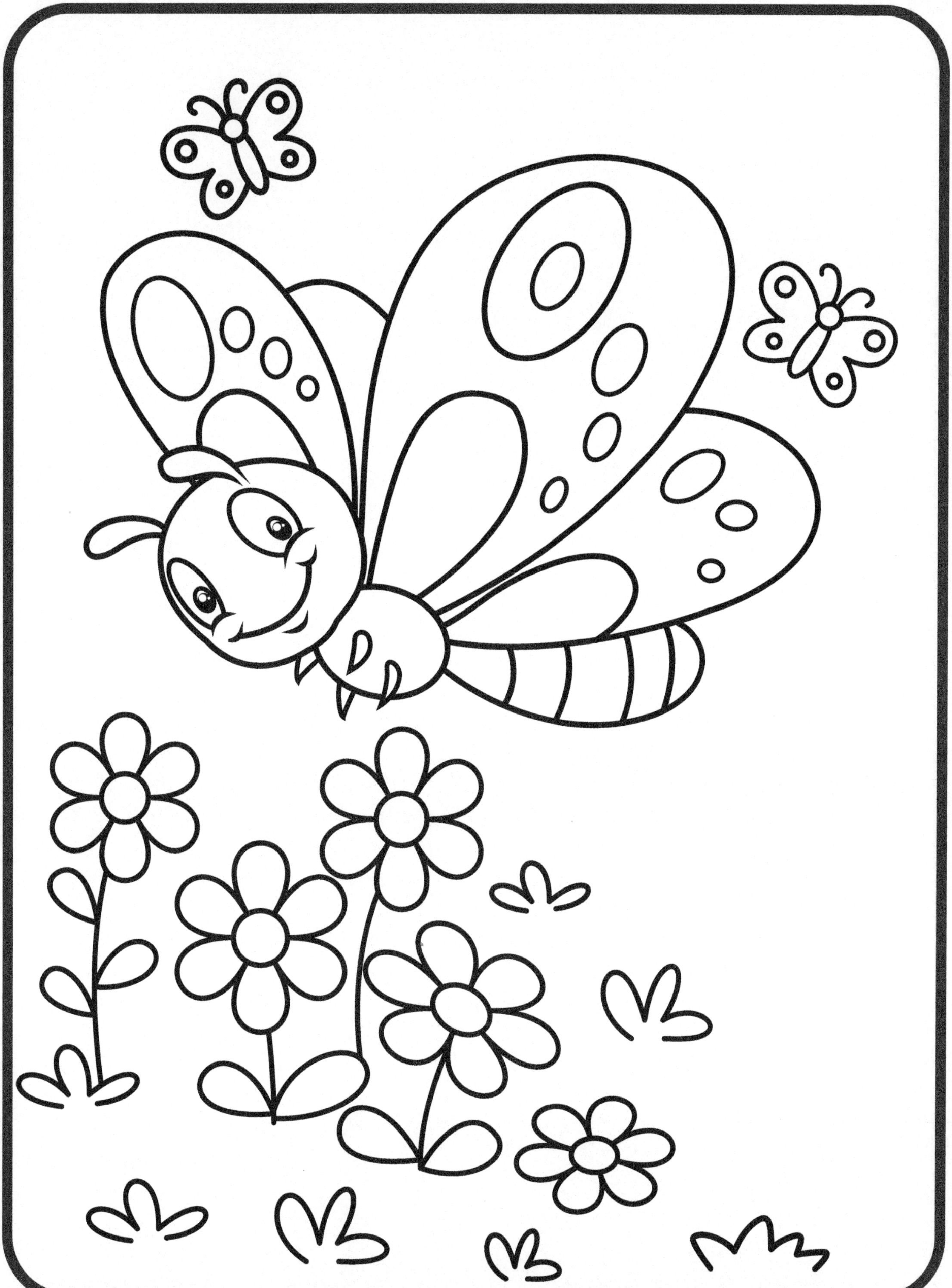

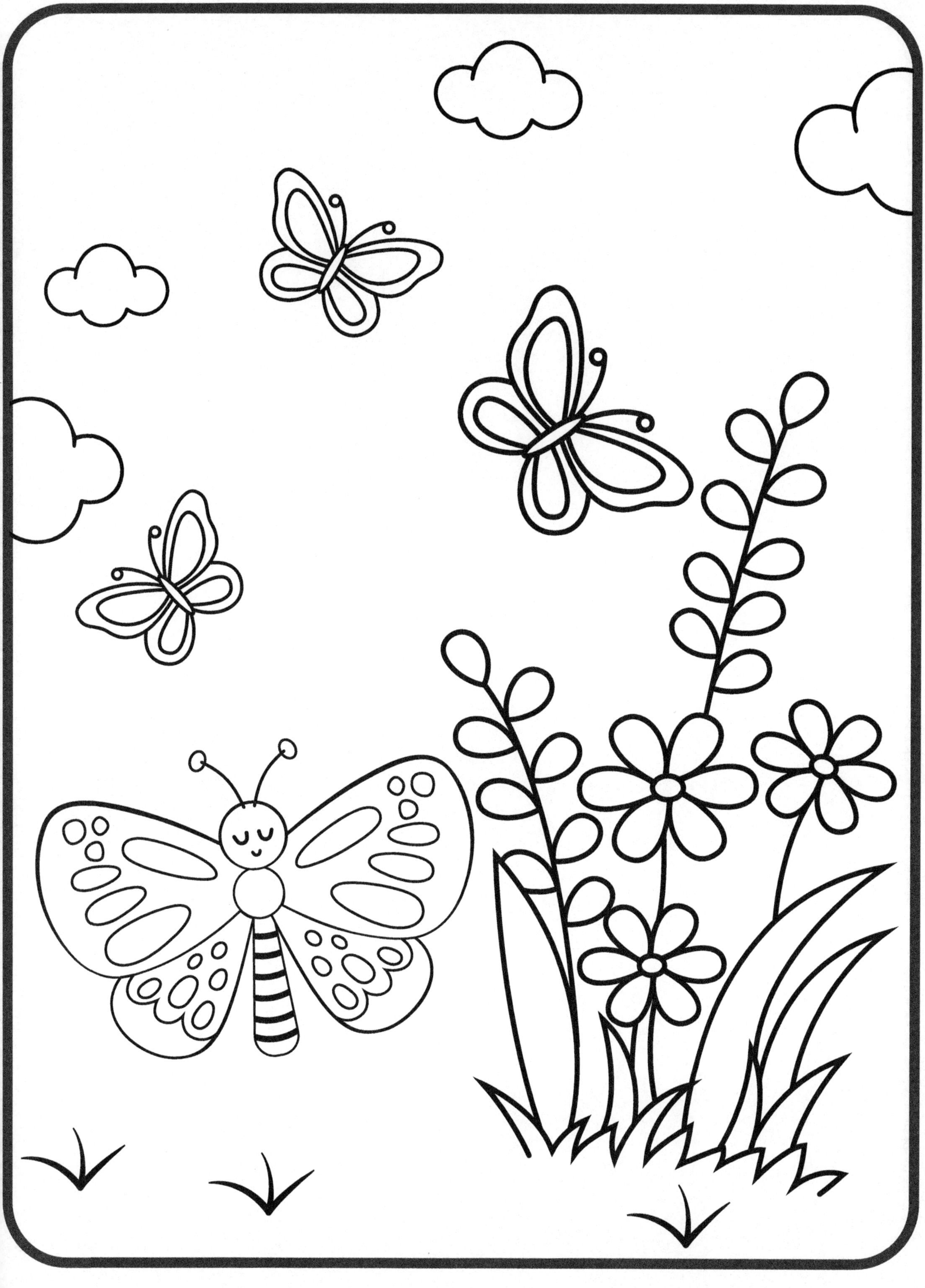

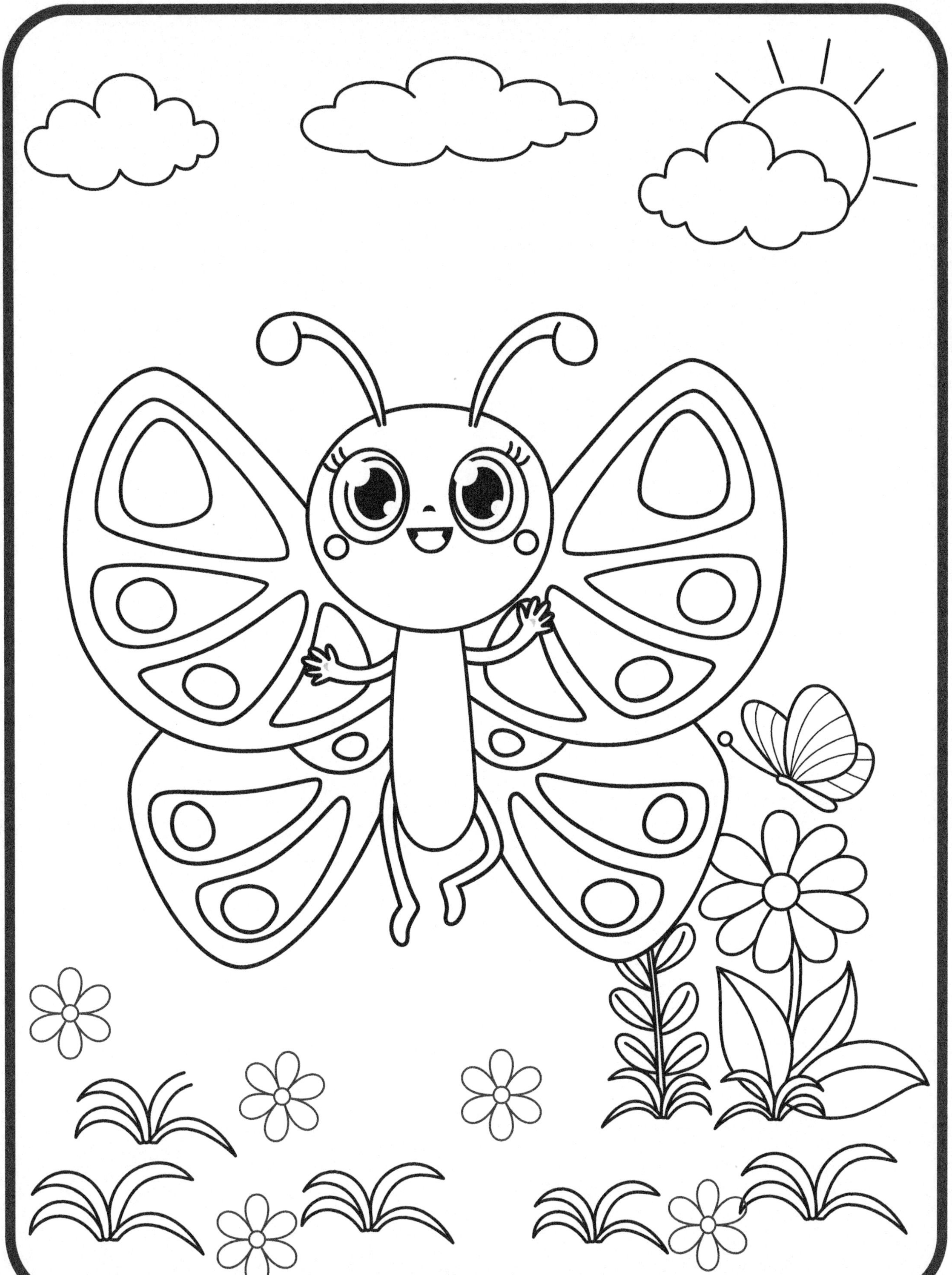

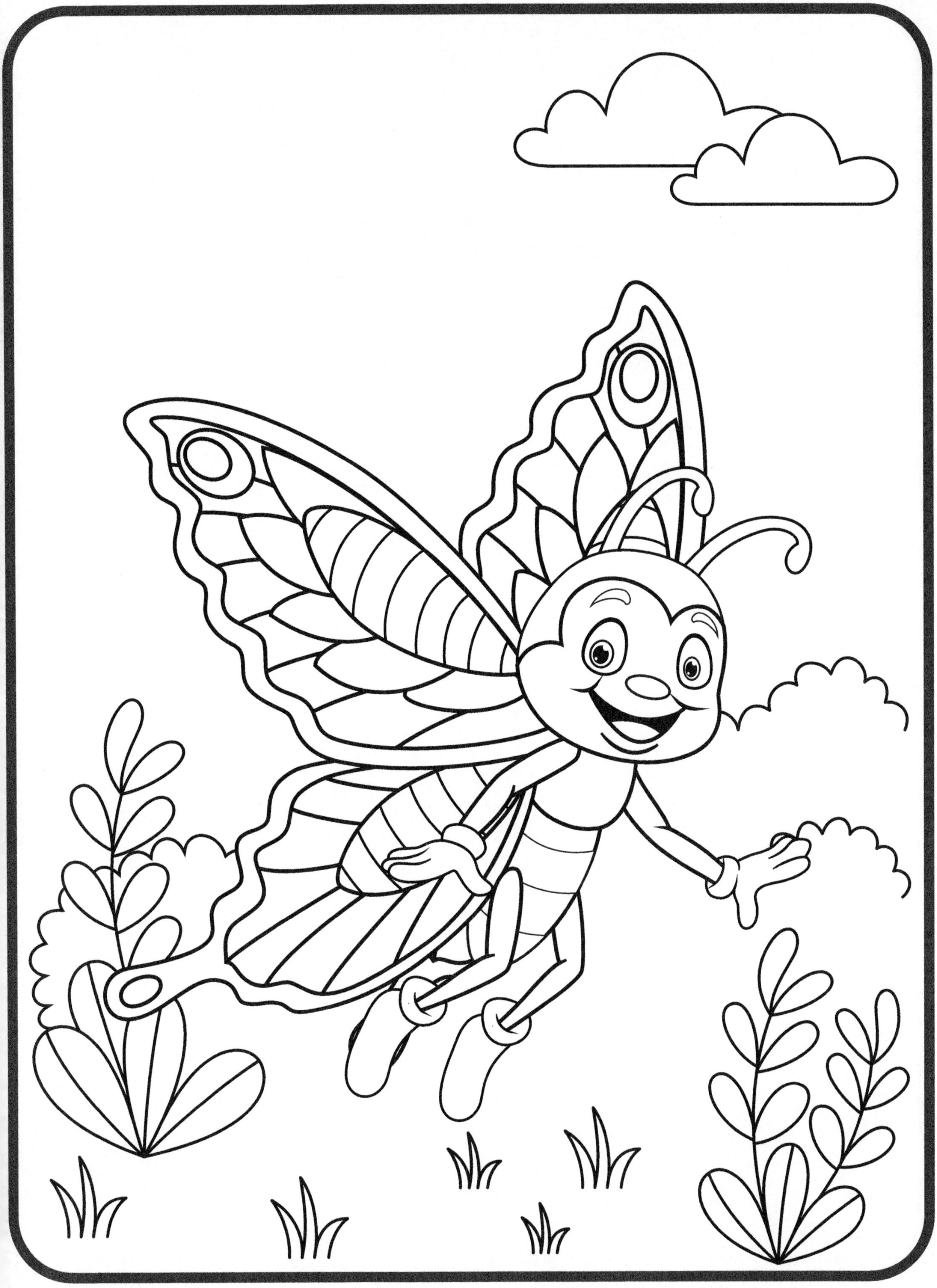

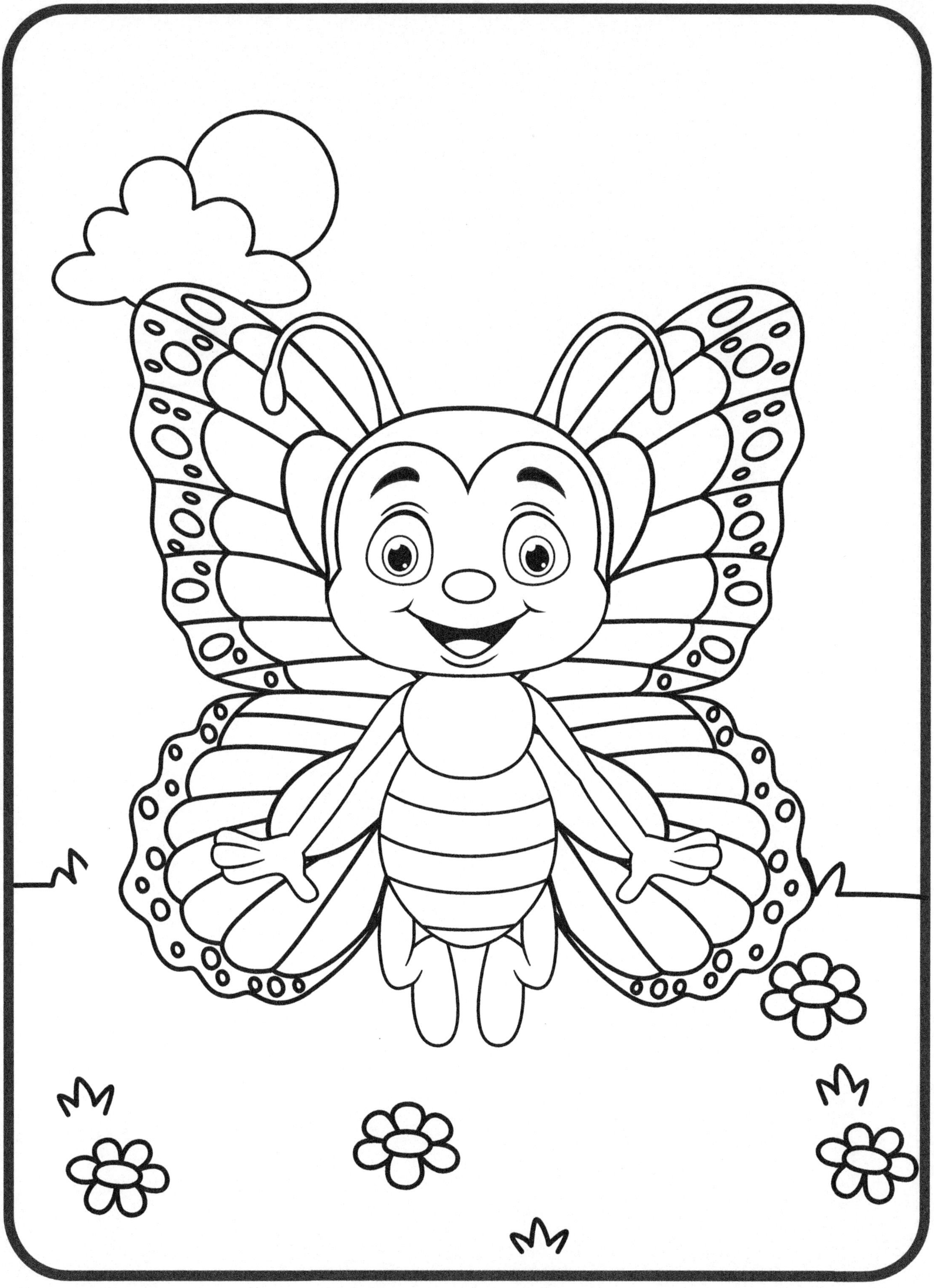

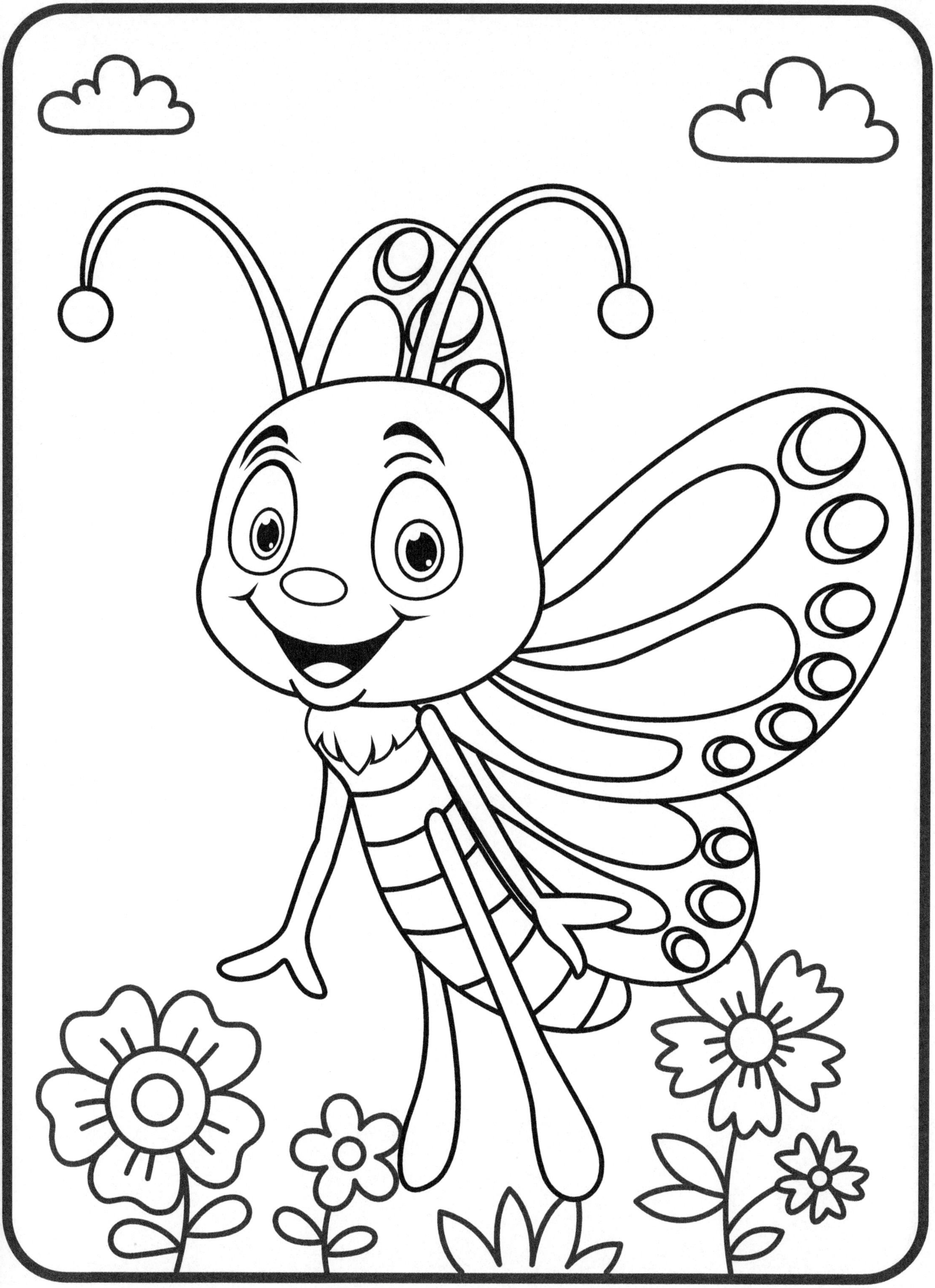

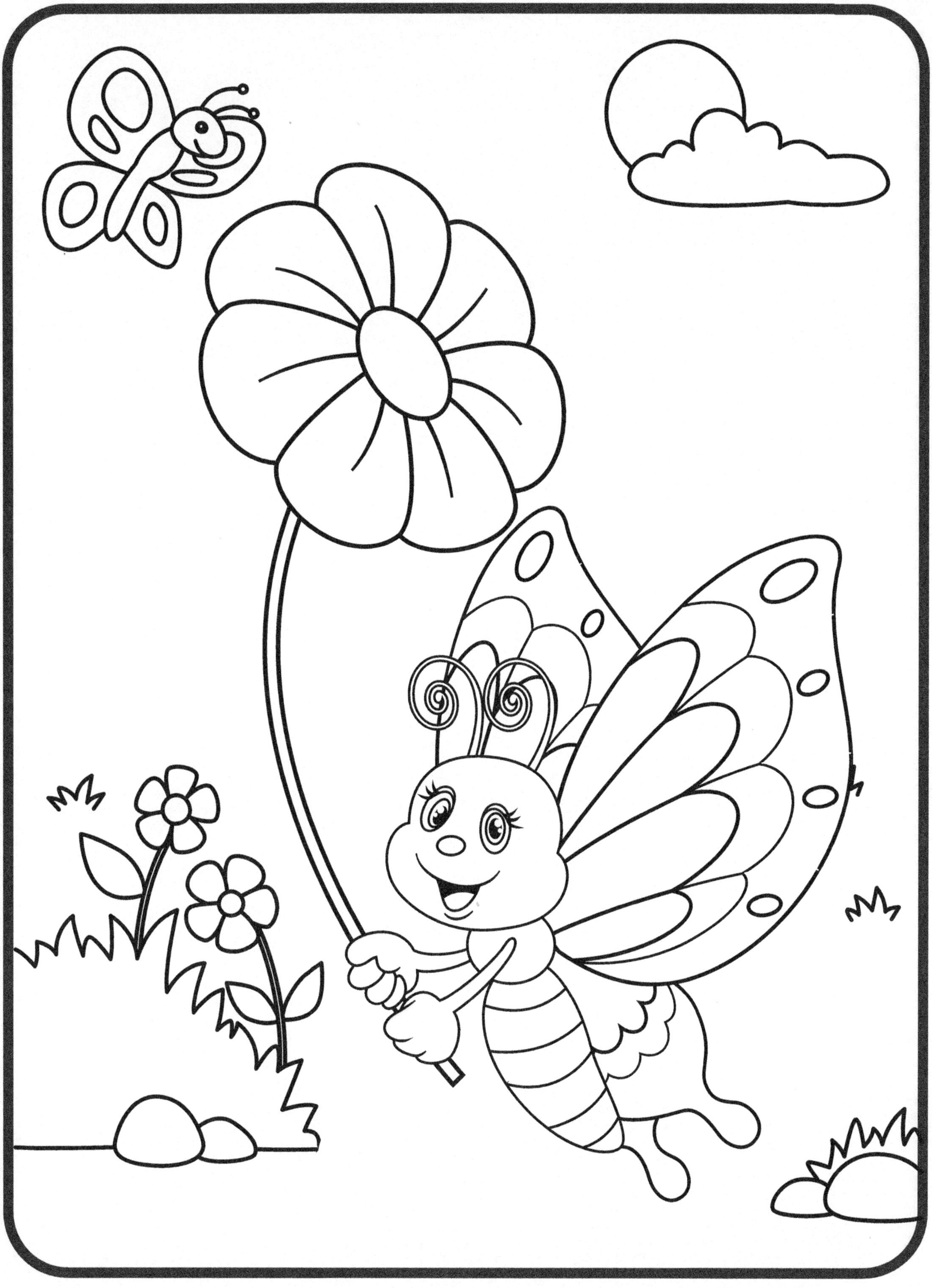

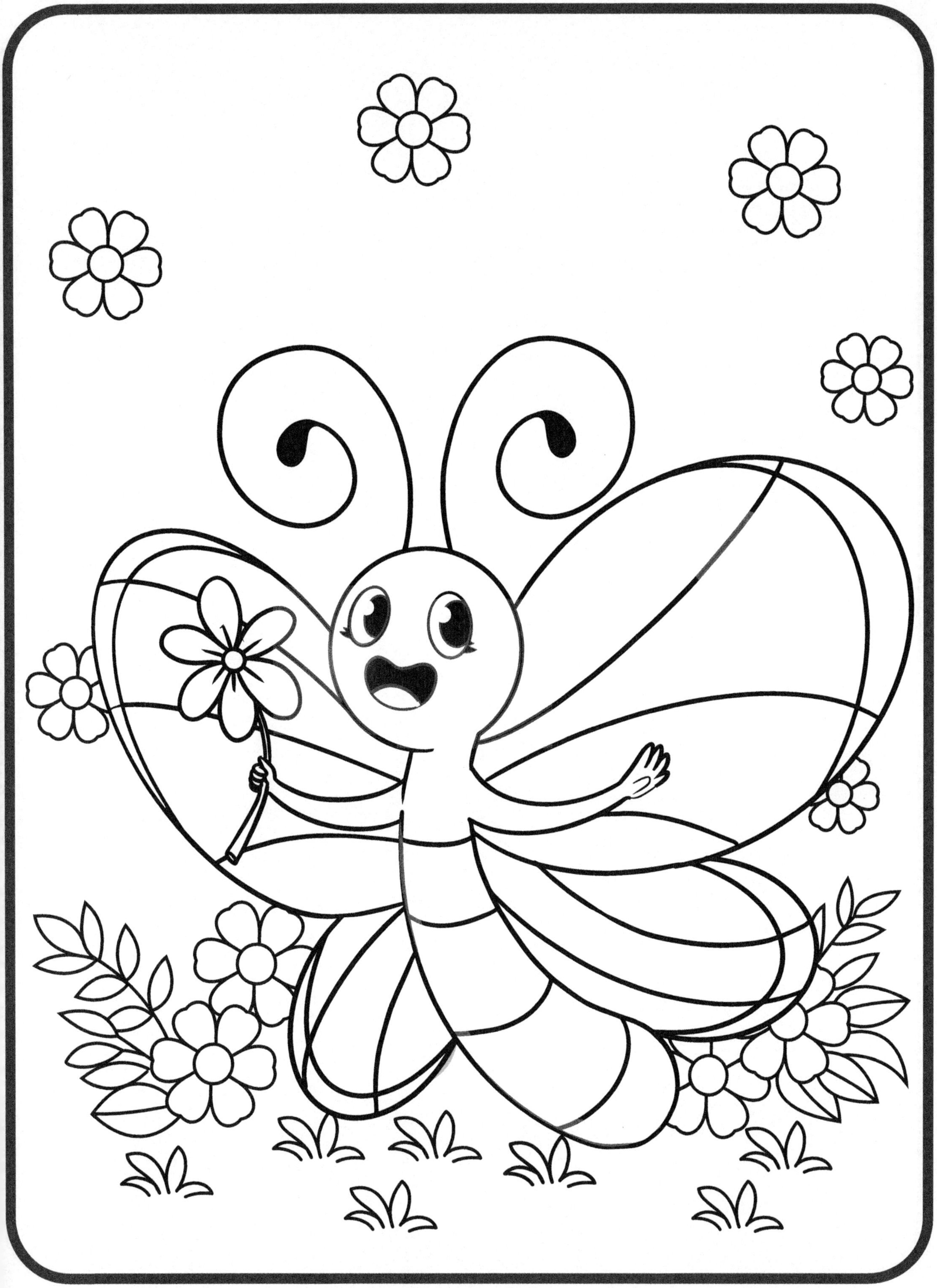

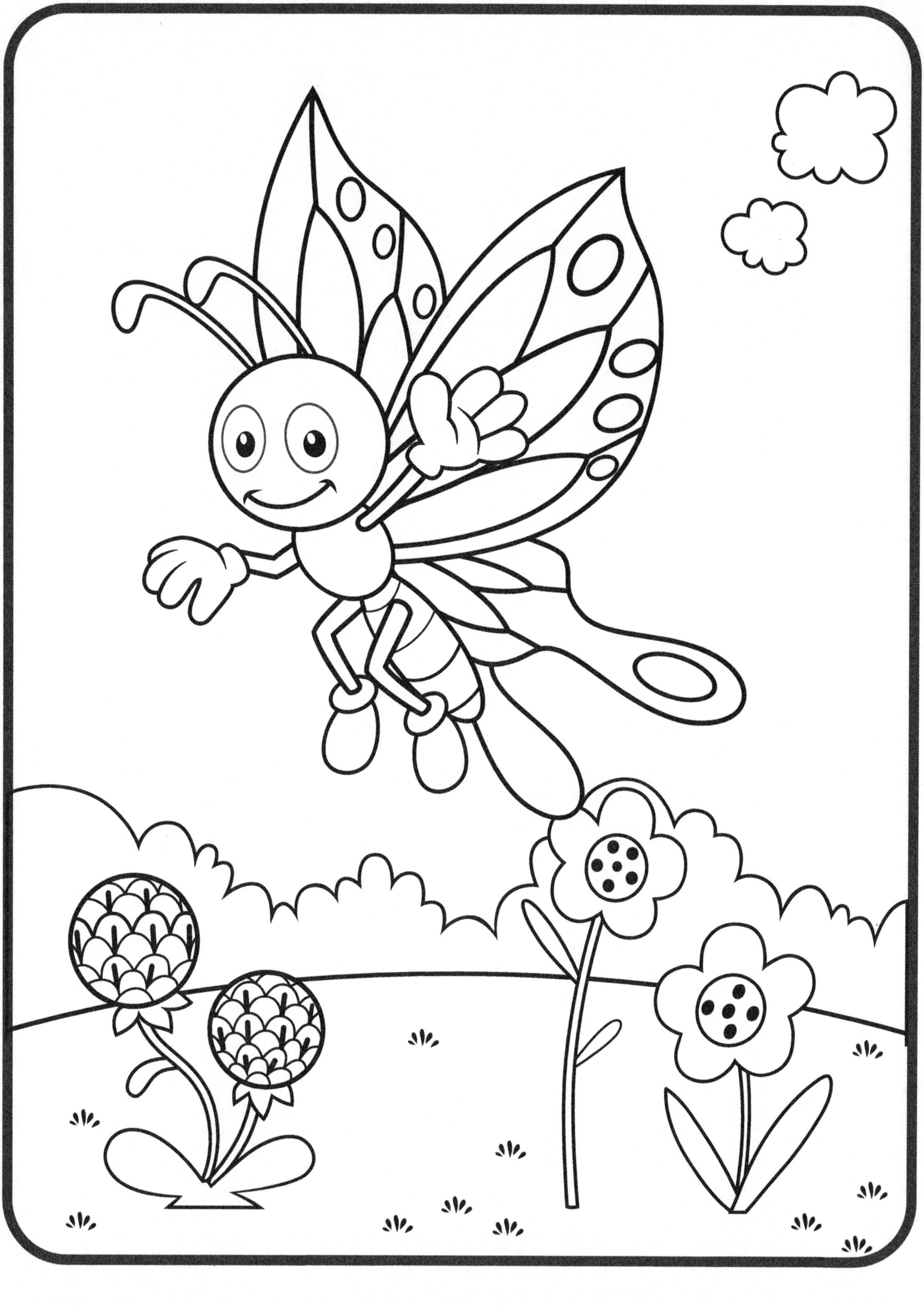

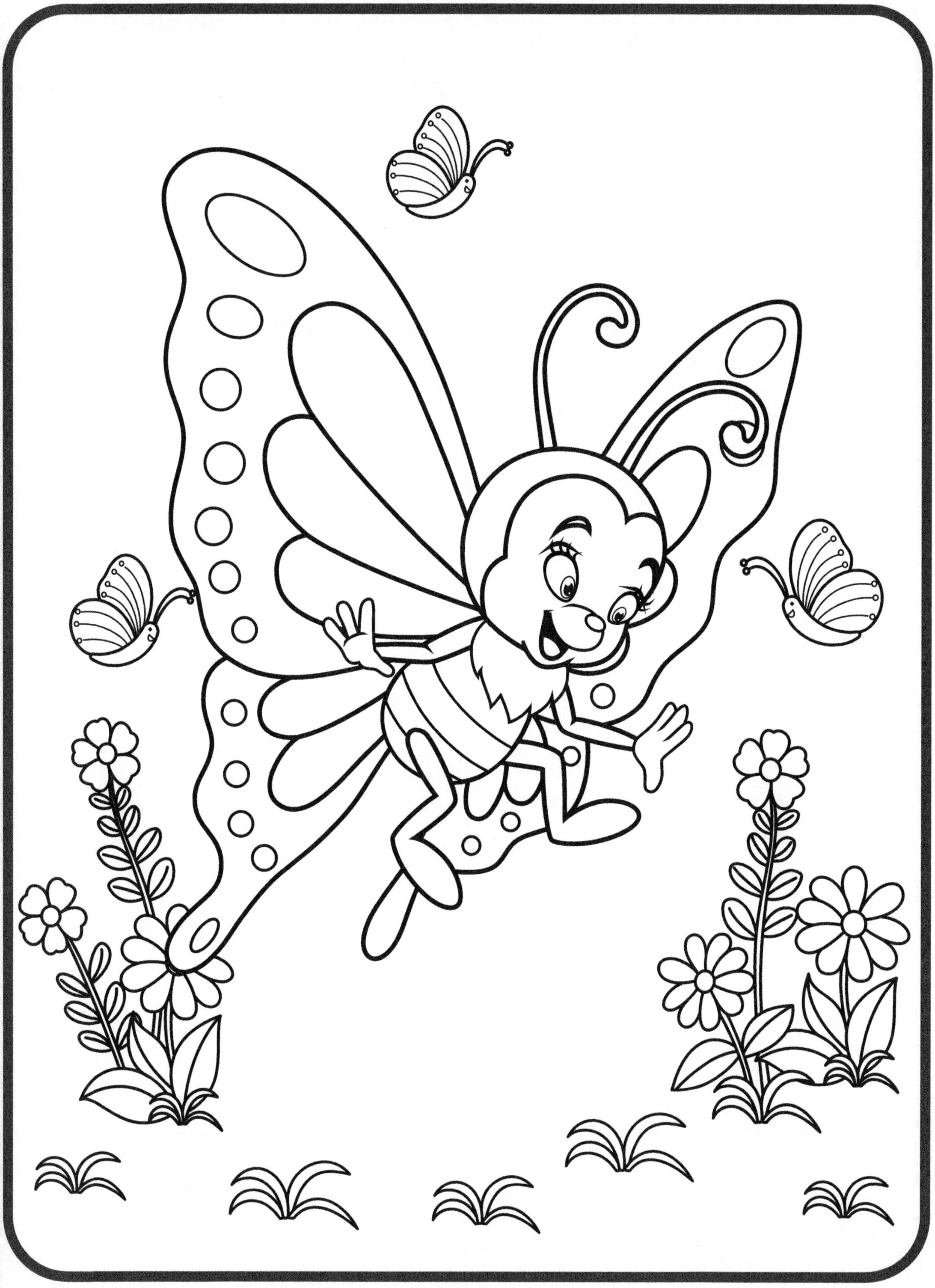

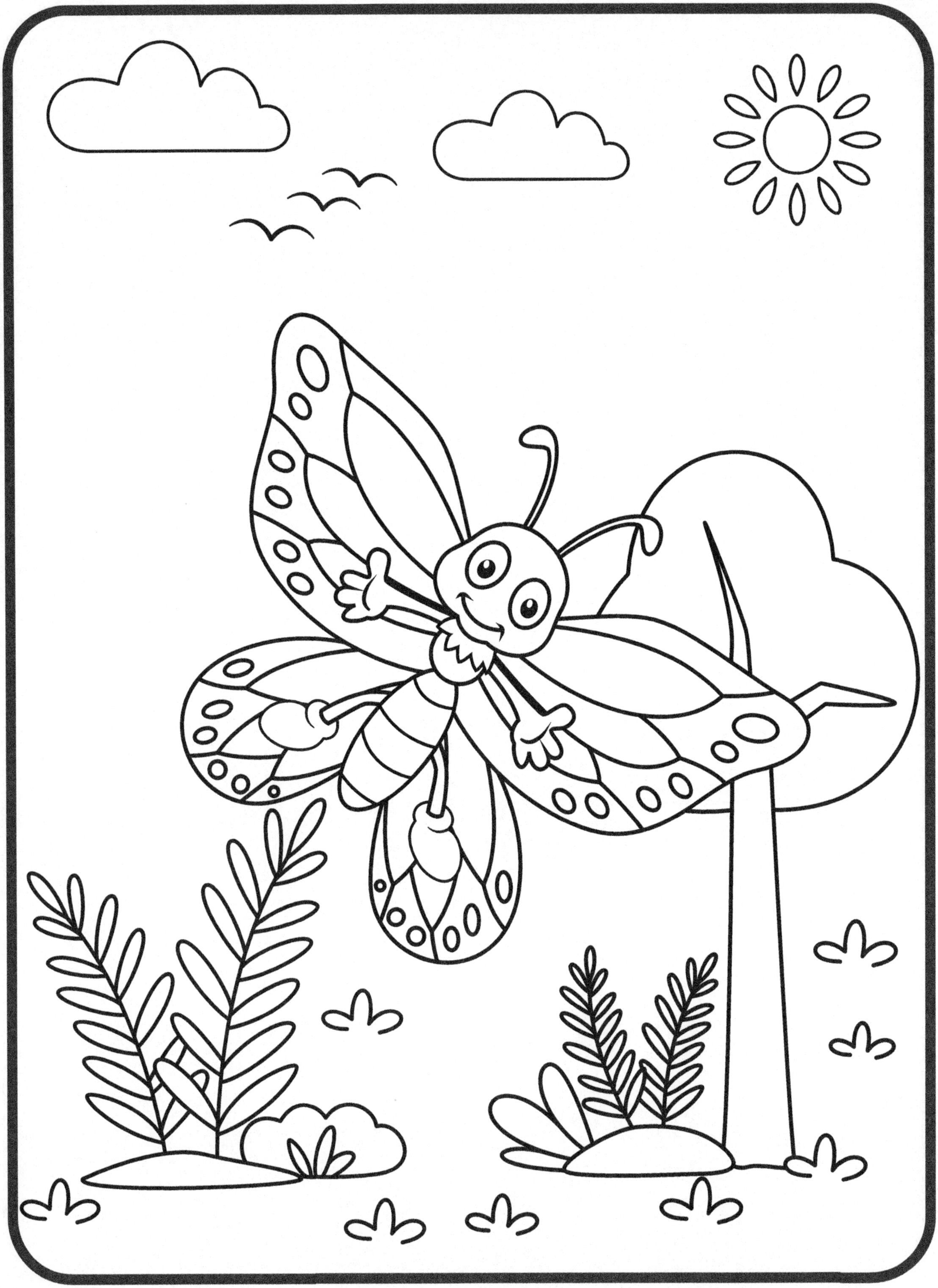

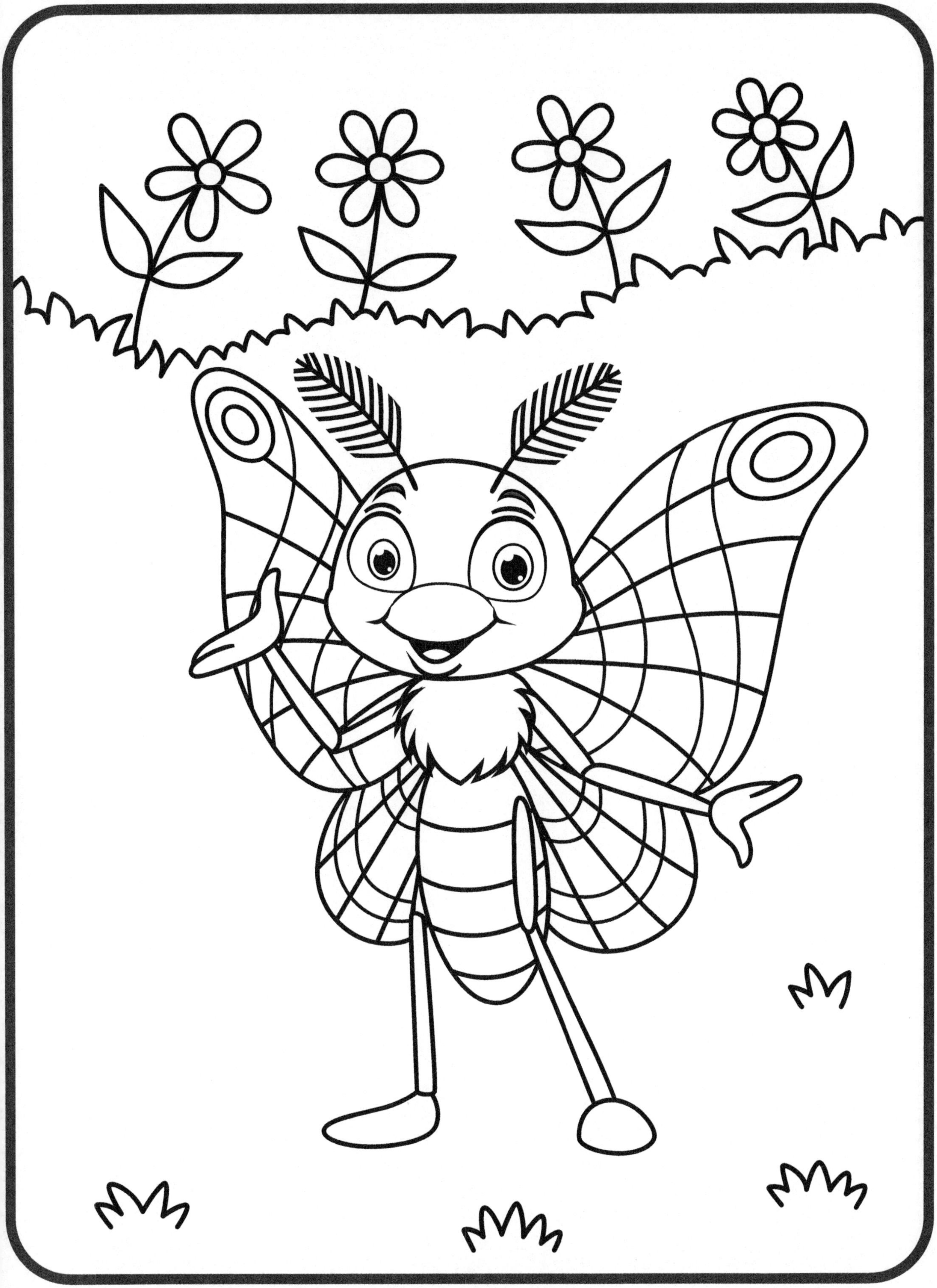

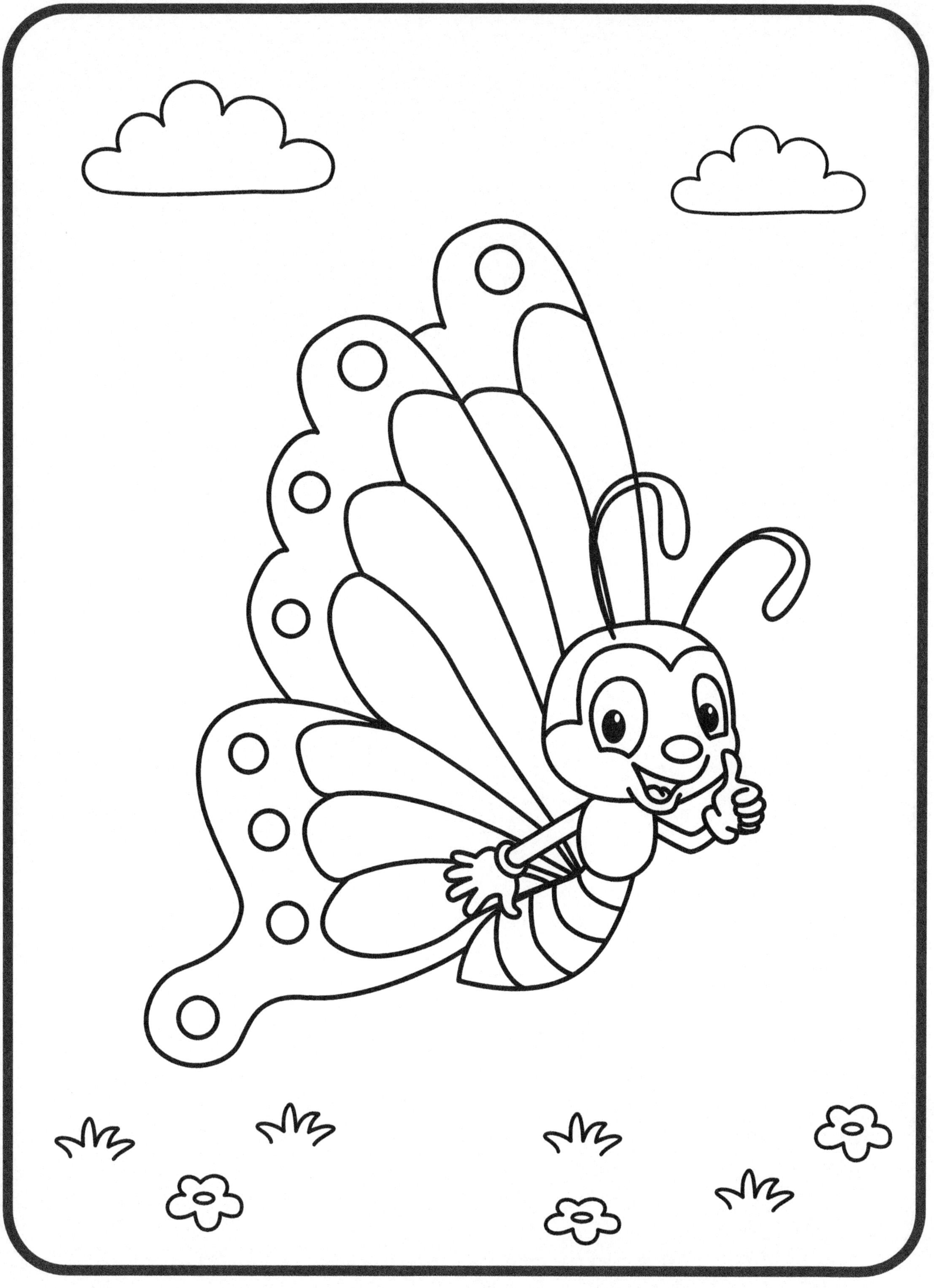

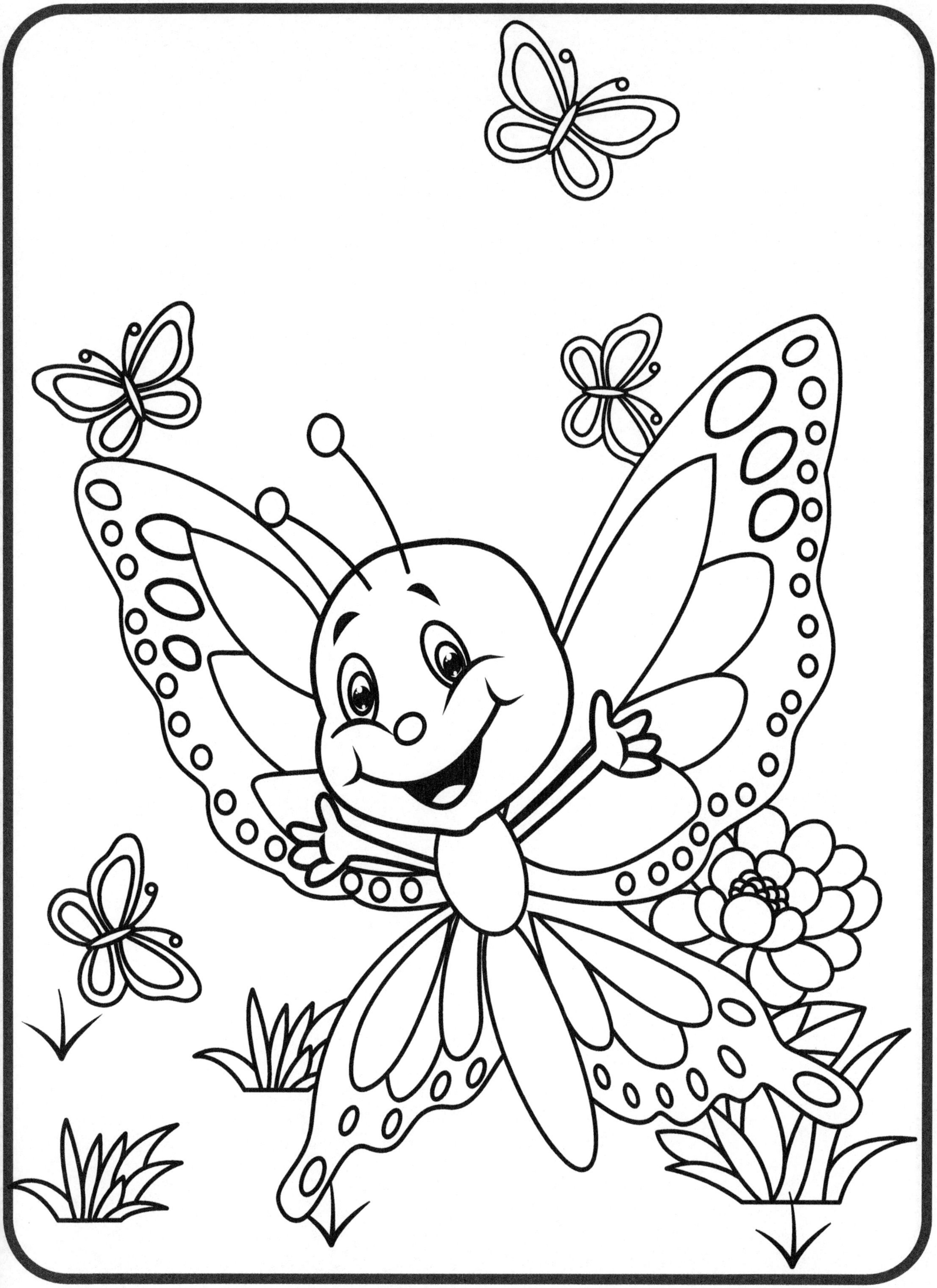

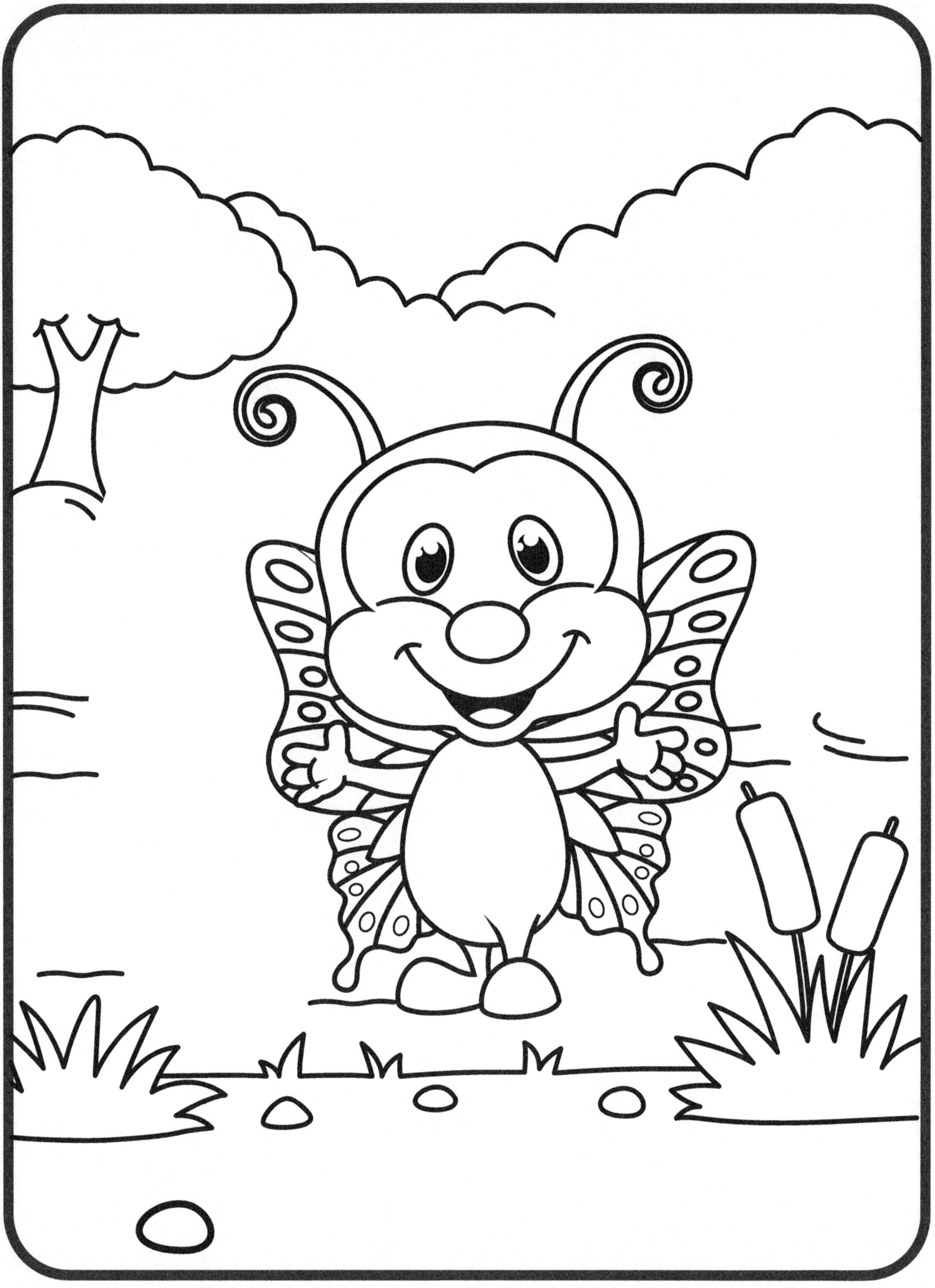

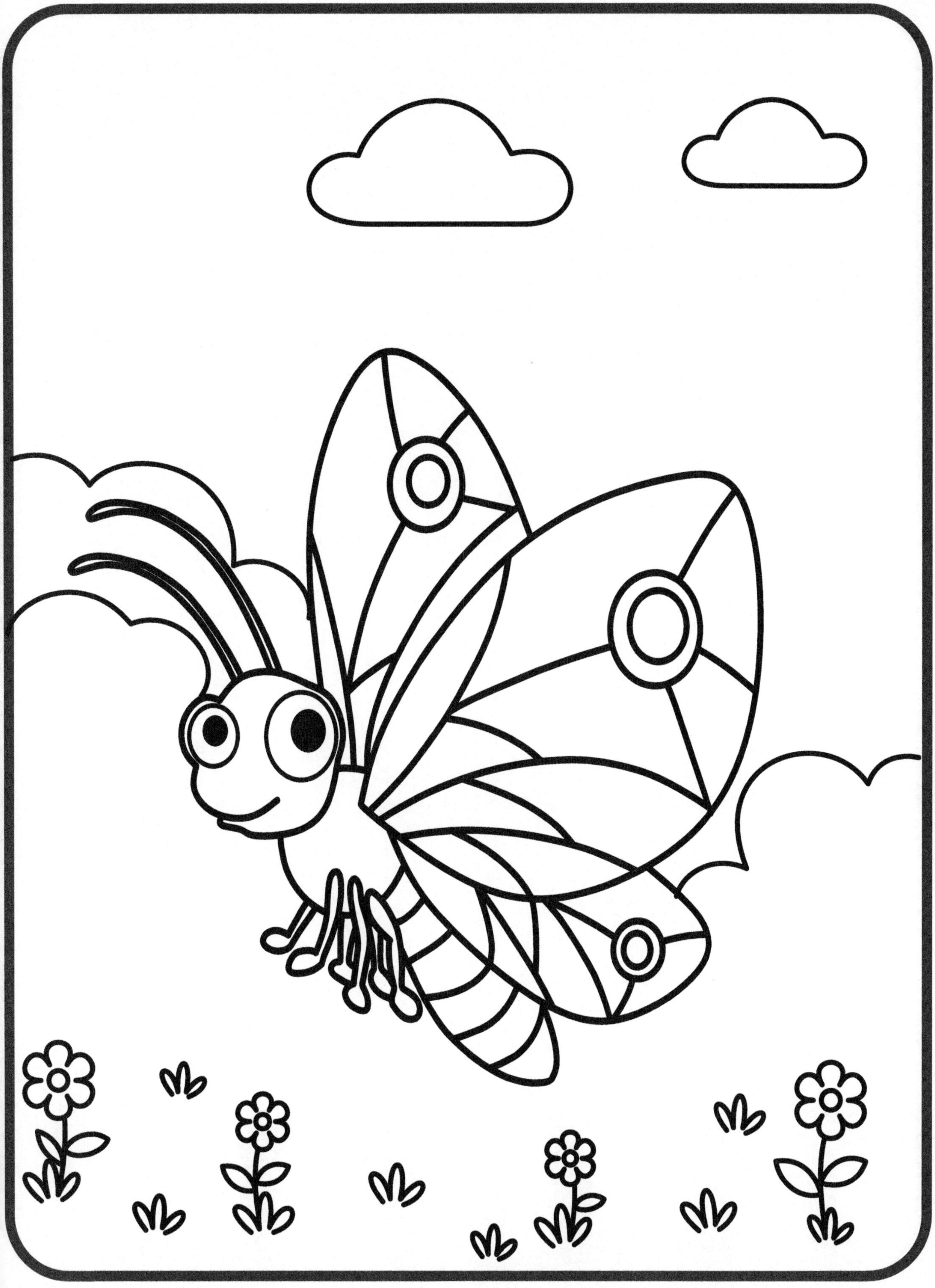

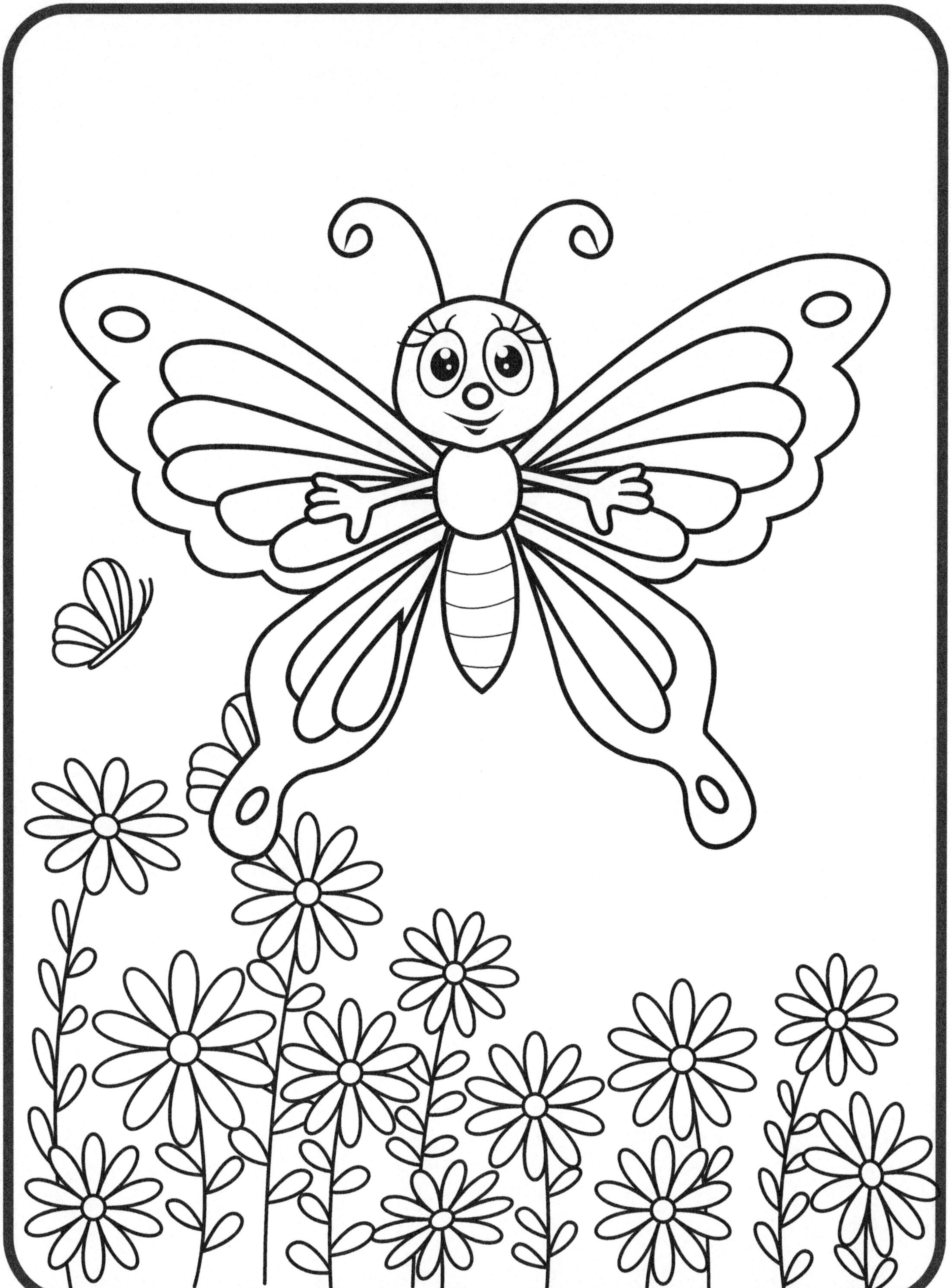

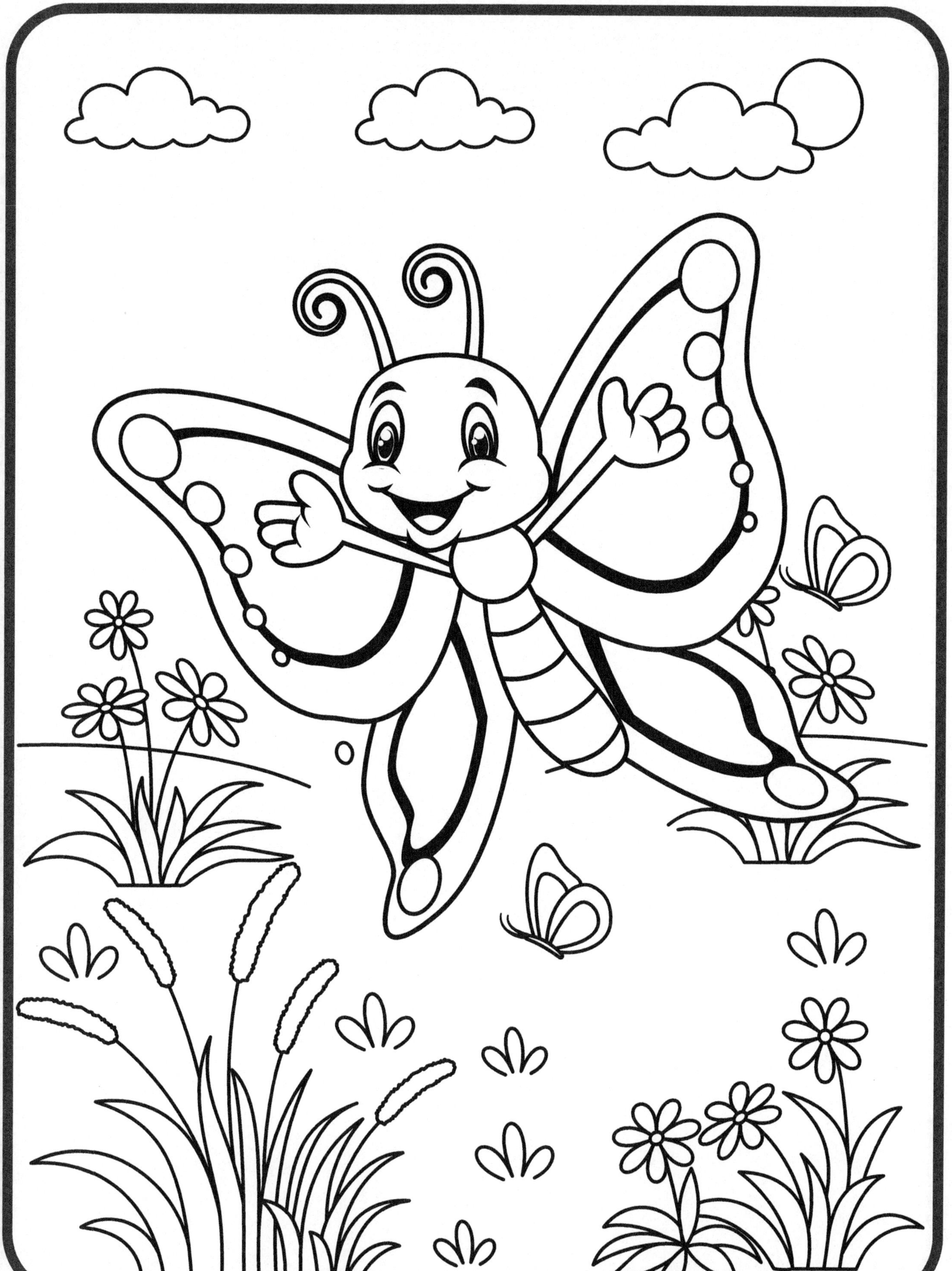

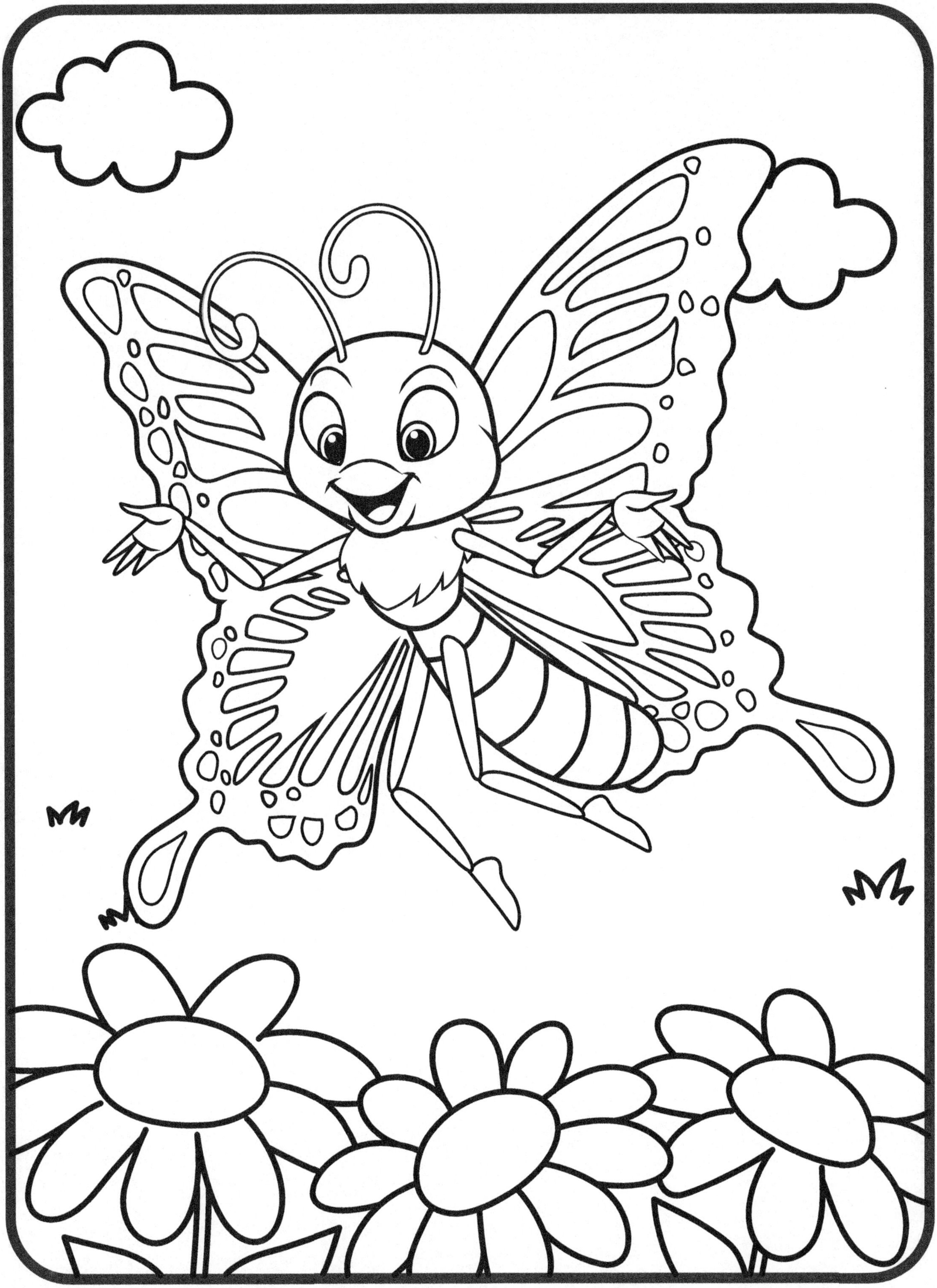

Printed in Great Britain
by Amazon

53565156R00037